Florida Laws

Digest and compilation of the school laws of the state of Florida

Florida Laws

Digest and compilation of the school laws of the state of Florida

ISBN/EAN: 9783337107963

Printed in Europe, USA, Canada, Australia, Japan

Cover: Foto ©Suzi / pixelio.de

More available books at **www.hansebooks.com**

DIGEST

School Laws

OF THE

STATE OF FLORIDA,

WITH THE

Forms, Regulations and Instructions of the
Department of Education.

WILLIAM N. SHEATS,

SUPERINTENDENT OF PUBLIC INSTRUCTION.

TALLAHASSEE, FLA.:
TALLAHASSEEAN BOOK AND JOB PRINT.
1899.

State Board of Education.

Constitution of Florida.

ARTICLE XII.

SECTION 1. The Legislature shall provide for a uniform system of public free schools, and shall provide for the liberal maintenance of the same.

Duty of Legislature.

SEC. 2. There shall be a Superintendent of Public Instruction, whose duties shall be prescribed by law, and whose term of office shall be four years and until the election and qualification of his successor.

Term of Sup Pub. Inst.

SEC 3. The Governor, Secretary of State, Attorney-General, State Treasurer, and State Superintendent of Public Instruction shall constitute a body corporate, to be known as the State Board of Education of Florida, of which the Governor shall be President, and the Superintendent of Public Instruction Secretary. This Board shall have power to remove any subordinate school officer for cause, upon notice to the incumbent; and shall have the management and investment of all State School Funds under such regulations as may be prescribed by law, and such supervision of schools of higher grades as the law shall provide.

Personnel of State Board Education.

Power of removal.

SEC. 4. The State School Fund, the interest of which shall be exclusively applied to the support and maintenance of public free schools, shall be derived from the following sources:

Interest only to be applie

The proceeds of all lands that have been or may hereafter be granted to the State by the United States for public school purposes.

Sources of State School Fund.

Donations to the State when the purpose is not specified.

Appropriations by the State.

The proceeds of escheated property.*

Twenty-five per cent. of the sales of public lands which are now or may hereafter be owned by the State.

*As amended in 1894.

1899.

Principal in-
violate.

SEC. 5. The principal of the State School Fund shall remain sacred and inviolate.

One Mill Tax.

SEC. 6. A special tax of one mill on the dollar of all taxable property in the State, in addition to the other means provided, shall be levied and apportioned annually for the support and maintenance of public free schools.

Basis of appor-
tionment of
Interest and
One Mill Tax
(as amended in
1894).

SEC. 7. Provision shall be made by law for the apportionment and distribution of the interest on the State School Fund and all other means provided, including the special tax for the support and maintenance of public free schools, among the several counties of the State in proportion to the average attendance upon schools in the said counties respectively.[*]

County School
Tax.

SEC. 8. Each county shall be required to assess and collect annually for the support of public free schools therein, a tax of not less than three mills nor more than five mills on the dollar on all taxable property in the same.

County School
Fund; whence
derived and
how disbursed
(as amended
in 1894).

SEC. 9. The County School Fund shall consist, in addition to the tax provided for in section eight of this Article, of the proportion of the interest of the State School Fund and of the one mill State tax apportioned to the county; all capitation taxes collected within the county; and shall be disbursed by the County Board of Public Instruction solely for the maintenance and support of public free schools.

Provisions for
School Dis-
tricts.

School Trus-
tees.

District Tax.

SEC. 10. The Legislature may provide for the division of any county or counties into convenient school districts; and for the election bi-ennially of three school trustees, who shall hold their office for two years, and who shall have the supervision of all the schools within the district; and for the levying and collection of a district school tax, for the exclusive use of public free schools, within the district, whenever a majority of the qualified electors thereof that pay a tax on real or personal property shall vote in favor of such levy; *Provided,* That any tax authorized by this section shall not exceed three mills on the dollar in any one year on the taxable property of the district.

Town or city
may be a
School Dis-
trict.

Disbursement
of District
Fund.

SEC. 11. Any incorporated town or city may constitute a School District. The fund raised by section ten may be expended in the district where levied for building or repairing school houses, for the purpose of school libraries and text-books, for salaries of teachers, or for other educational purposes, so that the distribution among all the schools of the district be equitable.

_____

*As amended in 1894.

Sec. 12. White and colored children shall not be taught in the same school, but impartial provision shall be made for both.

Separate schools for t groes.

Sec. 13. No law shall be enacted authorizing the diversion or the lending of any county or district school funds, or the appropriation of any part of the permanent or available school fund to any other than school purposes; nor shall the same, or any part thereof, be appropriated to or used for the support of any sectarian school.

Prohibitions on School Fund.

Sec. 14. The Legislature at its first session shall provide for the establishment, maintenance and management of such Normal Schools, not to exceed two, as the interests of public education may demand.

Normal Schools.

Sec. 15. The compensation of all county school officers shall be paid from the school fund of their respective counties, and all other county officers receiving stated salaries shall be paid from the general funds of their respective counties.

Compensati of school officers.

ARTICLE IV.

Sec. 25. The Superintendent of Public Instruction shall have supervision of all matters pertaining to public instruction; the supervision of State buildings devoted to educational purposes, and perform such other duties as the Legislature may provide by law.

Powers and duties of St Superintend ent.
Sec. 25, Art IV., Const.

Sec. 27. * * [He] shall make a full report of his official acts, of the receipts and expenditures of his office, and of the requirements of the same, to the Governor at the beginning of each regular session of the Legislature, or whenever the Governor shall require it. Such * * [report] shall be laid before the Legislature by the Governor at the beginning of each regular session thereof. Either house of the Legislature may at any time call upon * * [him] for information required by it.

Shall make report.

Abbr. Sec. :
Art. IV., Con

SCHOOL LAWS

OF THE

STATE OF FLORIDA,

COMPILED

From the Revised Statutes, and the Acts of the Legislatures of 1893, 1895, 1897 and 1899.

GENERAL PROVISIONS AND DUTIES OF OFFICERS.

SECTION 1. There shall be established and maintained a uniform system of public instruction free to all the youth residing in the State between the ages of six (6) and twenty-one (21) years, as far as the funds will admit, as hereinafter provided.

A uniform System of Public Instruction, Rev. Stat., Sec. 225.

SEC. 2. The officers of the Department of Public Instruction shall be a State Superintendent of Public Instruction, a State Board of Education, a Board of Public Instruction for each county, a Superintendent of Public Instruction for each county, local School Supervisors and Treasurers.

Officers.

Ib. Sec. 226.

SEC. 3. All such officers who shall hold their offices by statute shall conform to the regulations of the Department of Public Instruction.

Subject to regulations, Ib. Sec. 229.

SEC. 4. They shall retain their offices during the faithful performance of their duties, but not to exceed four years at any time.

Tenure of office.

SEC. 5. They shall be subject to removal for incompetency, neglect of duty, or any cause which would disqualify them for the positions if not incumbents.

For what removable.

SEC. 6. No officer shall vote on a question fixing his own compensation.

When not to vote. Ibid, Sec. 230.

SEC. 7. A majority of any educational board shall constitute a quorum for the transaction of business.

A quorum. Ib. Sec. 231.

SEC. 8. Each county shall constitute a school unit; all subdivisions of a county for school purposes shall be designated as school districts; all school districts levying a school district tax shall hereafter be designated as special tax school districts, and all schools receiving any district tax, as special tax schools.

SEC. 9. Every school officer who shall be appointed under statutory provision, is required:

1st. Before entering upon the duties of his office, and within ten days after receiving notice of his appointment, to subscribe to an acceptance of the appointment and to pledge that he will faithfully perform the duties of the position, and to forward the same with his postoffice address to the State Superintendent of Public Instruction.

2d. Before receiving any school moneys or property of any kind, for safe keeping or disbursement, to give bond, with two good sureties, the bonds to be fixed and approved by the Board of Public Instruction for the county, the original to be filed in the office of the Clerk of the Circuit Court, and a certified copy to be held by the officer giving the security, to be produced when required.

3d. Any officer in charge of school moneys or property to be so disbursed, shall satisfy himself that the officer to whom he issues it has given bond as aforesaid, or be personally liable for any loss in consequence of such neglect.

SEC. 10. Every officer shall turn over to his successor in office, on retiring, all books, papers, documents, funds, moneys and property of whatever kind, which he may have acquired, received and held by virtue of his office, and take full receipts for them of his successor.

SEC. 11. It shall be a penal offense for any individual, body of individuals, corporation or association, to conduct within this State any school of any grade, public, private or parochial, wherein white persons and negroes shall be instructed or boarded within the same building, or taught in the same class, or at the same time by the same teacher.

SEC. 12. Any person or persons violating the provisions of section 1 [section above] of this act, by patronizing or teaching in such school shall upon conviction thereof be fined in a sum not less than $150 nor more than $500, or imprisoned in the county jail, for not less than three months nor more than six months for every such offense.

SEC. 13. All matters of difference which may arise between school officers and teachers, or other persons, under the operation of this act, shall be submitted to the decision of arbitrators. The proceedings and powers of arbitrators shall be as provided by law for other arbitrations.

POWERS AND DUTIES OF THE STATE BOARD OF EDUCATION.

SEC. 14. The State Board of Education shall consist of the Governor, the Secretary of State, the Attorney-General, the State Treasurer, and the State Superintendent of Public Instruction. The Governor shall be the President, the State Treasurer shall be the Treasurer, and the State Superintendent of Public Instruction, the Secretary of said Board. Said Board is a body corporate, with full power to perform all corporate acts for educational purposes.

How constituted. Ib. 234.

A body corporate.

SEC. 15. The State Board of Education are directed and empowered:

Powers and duties. Ib 235.

1st. To obtain possession of and take the charge, oversight and management of all lands granted to or held by the State for educational purposes, and to fix the terms of sale, rental or use of such lands, and to do whatever may be necessary to preserve them from trespass or injury, and for their improvement.

With regard to school lands.

2d. To have the direction and management, and to provide for the safe keeping and expenditure of all the educational funds of the State; with due regard to the highest interest of education.

With regard to school funds.

3d. To entertain and decide upon questions and appeals referred to them by the State Superintendent of Public Instruction on any matter of difference or dispute arising under the operations of this act, and to prescribe the manner of making appeals and conducting arbitrations.

With regard to disputes or appeals.

4th. To remove any subordinate officer in the department for incompetency, neglect of duty, or other cause which would disqualify a person for the appointment.

Removal of subordinate officers

5th. To keep in view the establishment of schools on a broad and liberal basis, the object of which shall be to impart instruction to youth in the profession of teaching, in the knowledge of the natural sciences, the theory and practice of agriculture, horticulture, mining, engineering and the mechanic arts, in the ancient and modern languages, in the higher range of mathematics, literature, and in usual and ornamental branches not taught in common schools.

With regard to higher education.

6th. To co-operate with the State Superintendent of Public Instruction in the management of the Department; and in the general diffusion of knowledge in the State.

To co-operate with State Superintendent.

SEC. 16. The [State] Board of Education shall invest moneys of the common school fund which it may now have, and which

To invest School Fund. Ib. 267.

1899.

from time to time may come to its hands, in bonds of the United States and of the several States at the current market values of such bonds at the time of making such investments, and such Board may from time to time change investments held by it, and re-invest the proceeds arising from such change in securities authorized by law; *Provided, however,* That in no case shall any investment be made in any bonds on which the interest is not regularly paid, or as to the validity of which any suit may be pending.

In what may invest.

To fill vacancies on County Boards.
Abbr. sec. 4, chap. 4193.

Sec. 17. All vacancies on said Board [County Boards of Public Instruction] shall be filled for the unexpired term by appointment by the State Board of Education on the nomination of the State Superintendent of Public Instruction.

STATE NORMAL SCHOOLS.

Normal School for whites

Sec. 18. A Normal School for the training and instruction of white teachers is established at DeFuniak Springs, Walton county, under the direction and control of the State Board of Education.

Faculty, how elected.
Rev. Stat. Sec. 268.

The State Board of Education shall elect a faculty, to consist of a principal and two assistant instructors, who shall have in charge the training and instruction of all students, subject to the approval of the State Board of Education.

Normal School for negroes.
Ib., Sec. 269.

Sec. 19. A Normal School for colored teachers is established at Tallahassee, Leon county, similar in all respects as prescribed above for the establishment of the Normal School for white teachers, and subject to the direction and control of the State Board of Education.

SOUTH FLORIDA MILITARY AND EDUCATIONAL INSTITUTE.

Establishment.
Sec. 1. chap. 4334, May 29, 1895.

Sec. 20. The South Florida Military and Educational Institute is hereby established at Bartow, Polk county, Florida, under the direction and control of the State Board of Education, who shall elect such faculty as may be required to carry out the provisions of this act.

Design.

Sec. 21. The design of this institution is to teach such branches of learning, including military tactics, as may be required by the State Board of Education.

Manner of selecting student for free tuition, etc. Chap. 4508. Sec. 1.

Sec. 22. The Representatives from each county in connection with the Senator representing said county shall be empowered to name upon competitive examination and in such manner as the State Board of Education may prescribe, one student for each county who shall be resident in said county to the said South Florida Military and Educational Institute who shall be entitled to receive the benefit of a full course of Instruction at said institute without charge for board, lodging, tuition, use of text books, washing, fuel, lights and use of arms and equipments. Said student to be subject to such rules and regulations as may be established for the government and direction of said institution.

SEC. 23. That for the purpose of carrying out the provisions of this act the sum of nine thousand dollars ($9,000) be and the same is hereby appropriated for each of the two ensuing years, commencing September 1, 1897, out of any monies in the State Treasury not otherwise appropriated. *Appropriation. Ib., Sec.2.*

INSTITUTE FOR BLIND, DEAF AND DUMB.

SEC. 24. The members of the State Board of Education are the Trustees of the Institute hereinafter specified, under the name of the Board of Managers of the Florida Institute for the Blind, Deaf and Dumb. *Board of Managers. R. S., Sec. 270.*

SEC. 25. Said Institute shall remain in its present location near St. Augustine, in St. Johns county, and shall be an asylum for the indigent blind and deaf and dumb in this State. *Location. Ib., 271.*

SEC. 26. Said Board of Managers shall provide for the education, care and maintenance at said asylum of all persons residing in this State, between the ages of six and twenty-one years, who may be blind, or deaf and dumb. *Duty of Board of Managers. (As amended in chap. 1362).*

SEC. 27. Any person entitled to admission into said Institute, or the parent, guardian or next friend of such person, may apply to the Board of County Commissioners of the county of his residence, and the County Commissioners, if satisfied that the person is so entitled to such admission, shall issue a certificate to that effect, upon which the applicant shall be received into the asylum. *County Commissioners to issue certificate of admission. (As amended. Ib).*

SEC. 28. Said Board of County Commissioners shall supply means of transportation of such persons to said asylum, and at the close of each session the Board of Managers shall supply means of transportation for the inmates to their respective homes and return at the opening of the next succeeding session. The same to be paid for out of the general appropriation for the maintenance of said asylum; those who have the means will be required to pay the necessary expenses, tuition excepted, of their children or wards. *Transportation.* *Who shall pay. (As amended. Ib).*

SEC. 29. Said Board of Managers shall provide for the inmates of said Institute necessary bedding, clothing, food and medical attendance, and such other things as may be proper for the health and comfort of said inmates. *What Board of Managers shall provide. Rev. Stat. 275.*

Employ teachers Ib., 276.

Sec. 30. Said Board of Managers shall also provide for the education of the inmates of said Institute, and shall employ such teachers as may be competent to instruct the blind, and deaf and dumb, and fit them for aiding in earning a support, and in sharing the enjoyments of life.

Report. Ib., 277.

Sec. 31. Said Board of Managers shall report to the Legislature at each session the condition and management of said Institute, the work done therein and the expenditures therefor.

STATE SUPERINTENDENT OF PUBLIC INSTRUCTION.

State Superintendent, jurisdiction of. Rev. Stat., Sec. 132.

Sec. 32. The State Superintendent of Public Instruction shall have the oversight, charge and management of all matters pertaining to public schools, school buildings and grounds.

Duties. Ib., Sec. 133.

Sec. 33. It is his duty and he is hereby empowered:

To print and distribute laws, forms, etc

1st. To prepare and cause to be printed and distributed gratuitously to Boards of Public Instruction, and other officers and teachers as many copies of the school laws, and such forms, instruments, instructions, regulations and decisions as he may judge necessary for their use.

To call Conventions.

2d. To call conventions of County Superintendents of Public Instruction, and other officers, for obtaining and imparting information on the practical workings of the school system, and the means of promoting its efficiency and usefulness.

To hold Institutes.

3d. To assemble teachers in Institutes and employ competent instructors to impart information on improved methods of teaching and conducting schools and other relevant matters.

To apportion school moneys.

4th. To apportion the interest on the common school fund and the fund raised by the one mill State tax authorized by Section 6 of Article XII, of the Constitution, among the several counties of the State in proportion to the average attendance upon schools in the said counties respectively of children residing therein between the ages of six (6) and twenty-one (21) years.

To make discretionary apportionments.

5th. To make such apportionments as may in his judgment be right and just, when the census and returns on which the apportionments should be made are manifestly defective or have not been received by him.

To decide upon appeals.

6th. To entertain and decide upon appeals and questions arising under this act, or refer such to the Board of Education for decision.

7th. To prescribe Rules and Regulations for the management of the Department of Public Instruction.

1899.

To prescribe regulations.

8th. He shall have a seal for his office, with which, in connection with his own signature, to authenticate copies of decisions, acts or documents, which copies so authenticated shall be of the same force as the originals.

To have a seal. Ib., Sec. 134.

9th. He shall reside at the seat of government of this State, and shall keep his office in a room in the Capitol.

To reside at Capital. Ib., Sec. 135.

10th. He shall prepare the questions for county examinations and distribute same to County Superintendents; hold written examinations for and issue State Certificates; may grant Life Certificates as provided by law; and may order county examinations on other days than those prescribed by law.

To prepare questions for examinations, etc. Abbr. Secs. 8, 9, 10, 20, Chap. 4192, June 8, 1893.

11th. He shall nominate to the State Board of Education for appointment persons to fill all vacancies for unexpired terms on County School Boards [County Boards of Public Instruction].

To nominate County school Boards. Abbr. Sec. 4, Chap. 1193.

12th. It shall be the duty of the State Superintendent to visit each Seminary at least once in each year, and he shall annually make to the Governor, to be by him laid before the Legislature at each regular session thereof, a full and detailed report of the doings of the respective Boards of Education, and of all their expenditures, and the moneys received for tuition, and the prospects, progress and usefulness of said Seminaries, including so much of the report of the Board of Visitors as he may deem advisable.

To visit Seminaries. Sec. 323, Rev. Stat.

Report to the Governor.

13th. To file and preserve the same [certified copies of the monthly lists of persons who have paid their poll taxes] in his office as a part of the public records and furnish copies thereof when requested by citizens of this State.

File poll lists. Abbr. Sec. 2, Chap. 4600.

DUTIES AND POWERS OF COUNTY BOARDS OF PUBLIC INSTRUCTION.

SEC. 34. Each Board of Public Instruction is constituted a body corporate by the name of "The Board of Public Instruction for the County of............, State of Florida," and in that name may acquire and hold real and personal property, receive bequests and donations, and perform other corporate acts for educational purposes.

A corporate body. Rev. Stat., Sec. 236.

SEC. 35. Each Board shall, before proceeding to any other business, complete its own organization. Then the chairman and secresary shall make and sign two copies of the proceedings of organization, and annex their affidavits to each that the same is a correct and true copy of the original. They

Organization a primary duty. Ib., 241.

1899.

shall file one copy in the office of the Clerk of the Circuit Court of the county, to be by him recorded in the record of deeds, and file the other copy in the office of the State Superintendent of Public Instruction.

Titles vested
in.
Ib., 237.

SEC. 36. The title to the school property of the school shall be vested in them and their successors in office, except in such sub-districts as provided for.

Pay.
Sec. 1, Chap.
1567.

SEC. 37. The members of the various County School Boards shall be paid from the county school fund for their services, two dollars per day, for each day's service, and ten cents per mile for every mile actually traveled in going to and from the county court house by the nearest practical route.

Secretary of.

SEC. 38. The County Superintendent of Public Instruction shall be Secretary of the Board.

SEC. 39. The County Treasurers of the several counties shall

Treasurer of.
Ib. Sec. 240.

be and the same are hereby constituted the treasurers of the school funds in their respective counties

Rev. Stat.,
Sec 242.

SEC. 40. Each Board of Public Instruction is directed —

To hold titles.

1st. To obtain possession of, accept and hold, under proper title, as a corporation, all property possessed, acquired or held

May dispose of
property.

by the county for educational purposes, and to manage and dispose of the same for the best interest of education: *Provided*, That nothing in this act shall be so construed as to prevent any sub-district [special tax school districts] from holding

Special tax
district property.

school property that it has, or may hereafter acquire, for school purposes, or prevent such districts from receiving their portion of money as set apart for school purposes.

To locate
schools.

2d. To locate and maintain schools in every locality in the county where they may be needed, to accommodate, as far as

School age.
Minimum
term.

practicable, all the youth between the ages of six (6) and twenty-one (21) years, during not less than four months in each year.

To appoint supervisors.

3d. To appoint one supervisor for each school on the recommendation of the patrons, whose duty it shall be to supervise the work of the school and to report to the County Superintendent of Public Instruction monthly the result of his observations.

To select
school sites.

4th. To select and provide a site for each school house of not less than one-half acre of ground in the rural districts, and as nearly that amount as practicable in the villages or cities; the situation to be dry, airy, healthful and pleasant, also reasonably central and convenient of access for all who should attend the school.

5th. To do whatever is necessary with regard to purchasing or renting school sites and premises, constructing, repairing, furnishing, warming, ventilating, keeping in order or improving the school houses, outbuildings, fences, land and movable property, procuring proper apparatus for the schools, grading and classifying the pupils, and providing separate schools for the different classes in such a manner as will secure the largest attendance of pupils, promote the harmony and advancement of the school, and establishing, when required by the patrons, schools of higher grades of instruction where the advancement and number of the pupils require them.

6th. To employ teachers for every school in the county, and to contract with and pay the same for their services; *Provided*, That schools shall not be located nearer than three miles to each other, unless for some local reason or necessity.

7th. To audit and pay all accounts due by the Board of Public Instruction.

8th. To keep accurate accounts of all their official acts, proceedings and decisions, of all moneys received, held or disbursed, of all property acquired or disposed of, in a proper set of account books, and a record of the state and condition of each school, and to report the same to the State Superintendent of Public Instruction when required. They shall also at the close of the scholastic year prepare an itemized report of all moneys by them received and disbursed.

9th. To prepare and file with the Clerks of the Circuit Court of their counties respectively, by the first Monday in August, A. D. 1895, a detailed and itemized financial statement in writing, showing all sums of moneys received on account of county school funds for and during the year next preceding, and from whom received, and from what source derived, and all amounts paid out during such year, to whom and on what account paid. What funds, if any, are on hand, and what indebtedness, if any, is outstanding. Such statement shall be certified by the Treasurer of the county school fund and attested by the County Superintendent of Public Instruction, and in all counties where a newspaper exists, the Board of Public Instruction shall cause said statement to be published; *Provided*, The cost of such publication shall not exceed ten dollars to be paid out of the county school fund; otherwise they shall have the same posted at the court-house and at three other public places in the county.

10th. To prepare and file with the Clerk of the Circuit Court of their respective counties by the first Tuesday after the first Monday in September, A. D. 1895, and by the corresponding Tuesday in each and every month thereafter, an itemized

General discretionary duties and powers.

To establish High Schools.

To employ teachers.

Three-mile limit.

To audit accounts.

To keep a complete record of official acts.

To report to State Superintendent.

To file an itemized financial report annually with county clerk

To publish or post the same. (Sec. 2, Chap. 4332).

To file monthly an itemized financial statement with county clerk.

1899.

financial statement showing all sums of money received during the month next preceding on account of county school funds, and from whom received, and from what source derived, all appropriations made by such Board, and for what purpose made. All warrants drawn by such Board, in whose favor and for and on what account drawn, describing such warrant by date, number and amount. All such monthly financial statements shall be certified by the chairman of the Board of Public Instruction for the county and attested by the County Superintendent of Public Instruction, and the said Board shall without delay cause the same to be published in a newspaper of the county, when any such newspaper exists: *Provided*, The cost of such monthly publication shall not exceed two dollars per month, otherwise they shall post the same at the court house and at three other public places in the county.

To publish or post the same. Ib., Sec. 3.

11th. To put in operation in the public free schools in their respective counties a uniform system of school books; but however, that the adoption of such system shall be gradual and not sooner made than the interests of the pupils and patrons may dictate; and *Provided*, That the entire adoption shall be consummated by July 1, 1901.

To adopt text books. Sec. 1, Chap. 4080,

12th. The selection of books to constitute such uniform system in each county shall be made by the County Board of Public Instruction of the county, who before deciding upon any book or books shall consult with the County Superintendent of public schools and at least three leading teachers of the county. Before any adoption shall be made at least sixty days' previous notice of the time and place such adoption will be considered published once a week for three successive weeks in some newspaper having a general circulation throughout the county, or in the absence of such newspaper to be posted in at least five different and conspicuous places in the county shall be given by the School Board; any adoption made hereunder shall last at least five years. The County Superintendent shall see that the books adopted are used by the pupils and the teachers shall not use any other books in teaching.

To consult Co. Supt. and teachers.

Term of adoption.

Sec. 2, Chapter 4680.

13th. Nothing in this act shall have the effect to interfere with or impair any entire or partial adoption heretofore made and now existing in any county of the State.

Sec. 3, Chapter 4680.

14th. To prescribe, in consultation with prominent teachers, a course of study for the schools of the county and grade them properly; and to require to be taught in every public

To prescribe a course of study.

school in the county over which they preside, elementary physiology, especially as it relates to the effects of alcoholic stimulants and narcotics, morally, mentally and physically; and all persons applying for certificates to teach shall be examined upon this branch of study, under the same conditions as other branches required by law.

1899.

To require Physiology taught. Rev. Stat. Sec. 242, 10th.

15th. To fix the compensation for the services of the County Superintendent of Public Instruction.

To fix pay of County Superintendent.

16th. To perform all acts reasonable and necessary for the promotion of the educational interests of the county and the general diffusion of knowledge among the citizens.

Plenary powers.

17th. To hold regular meetings for the transaction of business, by arrangement with the State Superintendent of Public Instruction, and to convene a special session on emergencies when requested by the County Superintendent of Public Instruction.

To hold regular meetings.

18th. To prepare on or before the last Monday in June of each year, an itemized estimate showing the amount of money required for the maintenance of the necessary common schools of their county for the next ensuing scholastic year, stating the amount in mills on the dollar of taxable property of the county, which shall not be less than three nor more than five mills, and furnish a copy of the statement to the Assessor of Taxes of the county, and file a copy in the office of the Board of Public Instruction, and the Assessor shall assess the amount so stated, and the Collector shall collect the amount assessed and pay over the same monthly to the County Treasurer, who is also by law School Treasurer, to be used for the sole benefit of the public schools.

To make an itemized estimate for the ensuing scholastic year.

Rev. Stat., Sec. 242, 14th.

19th. To select candidates for admission to the State College and Seminaries.

To Seminaries, etc.

20th. To appoint, prior to any authorized examination, three teachers holding the highest grade certificate among the teachers of the county as a grading committee; and to keep secret the names of persons comprising said committee until its work is performed.

To appoint Grading Committee. Abbr. Sec. 6, Chap. 4331, and Sec. 14, Chapt. 4192.

21st. To fix a school day to comprise not less than five (5) and not more than six (6) hours, exclusive of recesses, and the time for the opening of the public schools for each county; *Provided,* That all schools must begin so as to close before the last day of June.

To fix limits of school day and date for schools to open. Abbr. Chap. 4195 and 4196.

2

1899.

22d. To order elections for the creation of special tax school districts, for the selection of School Trustees, for fixing the rate of millage to be levied in such districts, whenever the provisions pertaining thereto in Chapter 4678 are complied with; to determine the result of all such elections, and to perform other duties prescribed in said Chapter.

23d. To sub-divide the county into School Board Districts, to file a certified copy of their action with the County Clerk and publish the same, as prescribed in Chapter 4193, Session Laws of 1893.

24th. To have school census taken, in case the County Superintendent of Schools shall fail to perform any duty imposed upon him by the preceding section [Sec. 48, Par. 16th], as and when the same is required to be performed, it shall be the duty of the County School Board to cause the same to be done as soon as practicable by some person or persons to be selected by such Board.

25th. To examine at least twice each year the books and records of the Tax Collector which relate to the collection of poll taxes and said Board shall require prompt settlement for poll taxes, assessed, together with those not assessed but collected. Any Tax Collector or member of a County School Board who shall neglect to comply with the provisions of this act shall be suspended from office.

SEC. 41. No Board of Public Instruction shall have power to enter into contract with any of its members, except for the purpose of obtaining school sites.

ELECTION OF COUNTY BOARDS OF PUBLIC INSTRUCTION.

SEC. 42. At the first meeting in July, 1894, the County Board of Public Instruction in each county shall divide their respective counties into three county School Board Districts so as to place in each district, as nearly as practicable, the same number of qualified voters, the lines of said districts being so drawn as to place each election district wholly within one or another of said county School Board Districts; and the members of the County School Board [County Board of Public Instruction] shall file in the office of the Clerk of the Circuit Court for such county a certificate of their said action, containing a description of the boundaries of said district, and naming the election districts comprising each county School Board District, which certificate shall be published in a news-

*See Sections 1, 3, 4, 9, 12, Chapter 4515, [No. 1] and Sec. 2. Chap. 4516 [No. 2.]

paper published in the county; or if there be no newspaper published in the county, then by posting at the county court-house door for four weeks thereafter. The County School Board may thereafter change the boundaries of any such districts at a meeting in July of the year of a general election, but such change shall be certified in the Clerk's office and published as required for fixing such districts in the first instance.

When districts may be changed.

SEC. 43. That at the next general election, and every two years thereafter, there shall be elected in each county in this State a County Board of Public Instruction, hereinafter mentioned as the County School Board, consisting of three members, whose terms of office shall begin the first Tuesday after the first Monday in January after such election, and terminate upon the qualification of their successors two years thereafter.

Election of School Board.

Tenure of office. Ib., Sec. 1.

SEC. 44. * * A County Board of Public Instruction consisting of three members, one member from each School Board District, elected from the several counties at large of this State, shall be chosen at the general election A. D. 1898, and at every general election thereafter, unless changed by law.

How elected. Abbr. Sec. 3, Chap. 4537

SEC. 45. All vacancies on said Board shall be filled for the unexpired term by appointment by the State Board of Education, on the nomination of the State Superintendent of Public Instruction.

Vacancies how filled. Sec. 1, Chap. 4193.

SPECIAL DUTY OF MONROE COUNTY BOARD.

SEC. 46. The County Board of Public Instruction of Monroe county are hereby authorized and required to employ a competent teacher to instruct the Cuban pupils of the San Carlos school, in the city of Key West, in the elements of the English language.

To employ teachers for San Carlos school. Chap. 4533, May 31, 1896.

SEC. 47. The said Board of Public Instruction shall make provisions for the payment of the salary of the teacher so employed, out of the common school fund of said Monroe county.

POWERS AND DUTIES OF THE COUNTY SUPERINTENDENT OF PUBLIC INSTRUCTION.

SEC. 48. The County Superintendent of Public Instruction is directed—

Duties of.

1st. To make timely inspection of the county, to ascertain the location in which schools should be established, the number of youth who would attend each, and the amount of aid

To inspect county. Rev. Stat., Sec. 246.

1899.

that the citizens of the neighborhood will contribute to encourage the establishment of a school.

To visit and examine each school.

2d. To visit each school at least once during each school term, and to make a thorough examination of its condition as respects the progress of the pupils in learning, the order and discipline observed, the system of inspection pursued, the attendance of the pupils, the mode of keeping the school records, the character and condition of the school buildings, furniture, books, apparatus and premises, the efficiency of the school Supervisor, the interest and co-operation of the citizens in regard to educational matters, and to give such advice as he may judge proper.

To give advice.

To awaken interest.

3d. To do all in his power to awaken an increased interest in parents, guardians, school Supervisors and teachers, with regard to the better education of youth in every respect, and the general diffusion of knowledge.

To confer with Supervisors.

4th. To confer with the school Supervisors frequently and see that they attend to their duties, keeping them supplied with a copy of the school laws, decisions, blanks and regulations of the department.

To select fit persons for Supervisors.

5th. To select for school Supervisors persons whose character, qualifications and sympathy with education specially commend them to those positions.

To keep record of each school.

6th. To keep a record by number, name and description of the locality of each school established, of the expenses incurred for, and of his visits of inspection to, the several schools.

To report names.

7th. To notify the State Superintendent of Public Instruction, immediately upon entering his duties, of the names and addresses of all county school officers.

To decide disputes.

8th. To decide upon questions in dispute which arise under the operations of this act, when submitted to him by the parties interested, and to refer his decisions to the Board of Public Instruction.

To look after school buildings and funds.

10th. To see that the interests of the county are properly guarded, and its rights secured in the making and performance of every contract for the construction of school buildings, or for other purposes; and that all moneys apportioned to or raised by the county are applied to the objects for which they were granted or raised.

To hold examinations, etc. Abbr. Chaps. 4192 and 4331.

11th. To examine candidates for teaching and to issue certificates, performing all acts in connection therewith as prescribed by statutes.

12th. To hold a special examination, and issue temporary certificates for a term of not longer than the interval between the regular examinations, provided the applicant for such certificate furnishes satisfactory reasons for having failed to attend the regular examination.

Special examinations.
Abbr. Sec. 9,
Chap. 4331.

13th. To revoke or suspend certificates, and to suspend those issued by other authority for cause manifestly sufficient, giving notice in writing to the authority issuing them and of the grounds for so doing; also notifying the teacher in like manner, and of the right of appeal, to whom and when such appeal should be made. *See Section* 72.

To revoke or suspend certificates.
Rev. Stat. Sec. 246.

14th. To receive from the Grading Committee, file and properly preserve in his office, for at least one year, all examination questions; and to publish in the newspaper designated by any dissatisfied examinee the questions and his answers to the same upon request and of said examinee.

To file examination papers, etc.
Abbr. Sec. 13,
Chap. 4192.

15th. Acting as Secretary of the County School Board, to make and forward monthly a certified copy of the monthly lists of persons who have paid their poll taxes, mentioned in Section 1 of this Act, [Chapter 4666] to the State Superintendent of Public Instruction, who shall file and preserve the same in his office as a part of the public records and furnish copies thereof when requested by citizens of this State.

To file poll tax lists. Sec. 2,
Chapter 4666.

16th. Before the 15th day of May in the year 1900, and every ten years thereafter, to take the census of all children in his county, between the ages of 6 and 21 years; and if any such children be idiots, or insane, or blind, or deaf-mutes he shall so state, and he shall report such census to the School Board of the county, and to the State Superintendent of Public Instruction, on or before the first day of June of the year in which such census shall be taken. He shall certify to such report, as being correct, and shall be paid three cents for each child so reported, and upon his failing to perform the duties herein required of him, he shall be relieved from office. In case he shall employ any person or persons to assist in making any such enumeration of such children, such person or persons shall make a sworn statement showing when and where such enumeration was made, and that the same is correct, and the same shall be filed by the Superintendent with the School Board as part of his report.

To take school census. Sec. 1,
Chap. 1699.

NOTE—County Superintendent not authorized to purchase lands for school purposes without being authorized by County Board of Instruction. Board of Public Instruction Nassau County vs. Billings, 15 Fla.. 686.

Two examina-
tions yearly.

Dates for.

SECTION 49. There shall be held two examinations a year in each county in the State, beginning on Tuesday after the first Monday in June and September, and each may continue one or more days at the discretion of the examiner and a vote of the examinees; *Provided*, That only one examination may be held in any county if two be found unnecessary; *Provided further*, That County Superintendents may hold a special ex-

Special exam-
ination. Sec.
9, Chap. 4331.

amination, and issue Temporary Certificates for a term of not longer than the interval between the regular examinations, provided the applicant for such certificate furnishes satisfactory reasons for having failed to attend the regular examination.

One examina-
tion at county
seat. Ib. Sec.
11.

SEC. 50. That at least one of the examinations of teachers shall be held at the county seat of the county in which the examination is held. *Provided*, That where two examinations are held the County Board of Public Instruction may designate another convenient place for holding one of such examinations other than the county site.

Special exam-
inations. Sec.
20, Chap.
4192.

SEC. 51. The State Superintendent, for sufficient cause, may order examinations held on days other than those prescribed by Section 19 [49 above] of this act.

Who County
Superinten-
dent to exam-
ine.

SEC. 52. Candidates for Third, Second, or First Grade Certificates shall be examined by the County Superintendent of Public Instruction on questions prepared in all cases by the State Superintendent of Public Instruction. The questions

Questions to
be sent under
seal.

shall be sent sealed to the County Superintendents of the various counties, which seal shall not be broken until the morn-

When to be
broken.

ing of the day on which the questions for that day are to be used, and then only in the presence of the persons assembled for examination. Any person or persons who shall be found

Penalty for
cheating.

guilty of securing or attempting to secure the prepared questions, or who shall furnish the prepared questions to any teacher or other person in any other way than prescribed by this act, shall be debarred from teaching a school or from holding any school office in this State. The candidates for

Procedure in
case of doubt
as to meaning
of question.
Ib. 10.

certificates shall ask no questions, nor receive assistance from any source during the examination. In case any examinee may be in doubt as to the meaning of any question, he or she may state in writing the point in doubt and answer accordingly, which answer shall receive due consideration in grading the papers.

Sec. 53. All examination papers shall be prepared in the presence of the County Superintendent or his appointed assistant, who shall collect the questions and answers on each branch as completed, and said examiner shall accept no paper of any examinee containing a name or mark which would indicate to any other than the examiner its author. Said examiner shall himself, on collecting each paper, designate it by a number known only to himself, and shall keep a record by number and by name of the author of each examination paper. Every examinee shall complete and hand in the answers on each branch before the questions on any other branch shall be given out. When every examinnee has completed all the branches, the examiner shall arrange and bundle together all the papers of each examinee and shall deliver the whole to a Grading Committee.

1899.

Mode of conducting examinations.
Ib. 11.

GRADING COMMITTEE.

Sec. 54. It shall be the duty of the County Board of Public Instruction, before every public examination, to appoint a Grading Committee, and to keep secret the names of persons comprising said committee until its work is performed.

County Board Board to appoint and to keep secret names of
Sec. 14, Chapter 4192.

Sec. 55. The County Board of Public Instruction, prior to any authorized examination, shall appoint three teachers holding the highest grade certificate among the teachers of the county as a Grading Committee; said committee shall, immediately after the close of any examination, carefully examine and grade each paper turned over to it by the County Superintendent. When the said committee shall have completed its work it shall deliver back to the County Superintendent all papers turned over to it, with a gradation sheet showing the grade of each examinee in each branch upon which he or she was examined, also the average grade and rank of each examinee. The County Superintendent shall then, for the first time, make known to the Grading Committee the names corresponding to the number of any examinee, and shall then, in the presence of said committee, present his list and write on said gradation sheet the name of each examinee after his or her proper number. The said Grading Committee shall retain one copy of said gradation sheet, and shall file one with the County Superintendent, who shall issue certificates to the examinees, making averages according to the provisions of Sections 1, 2 and 3 [62, 63 and 64 of this compilation] of this act, and to no others.

Who eligible.

Duties of.

Gradation sheet.

To retain copy. sec. 6, Chap. 4331.

1899.

To file papers
with County
Superinten-
dent. Sec. 13,
4192.

SEC. 56. All examination questions and answers prepared by the applicant for certificates shall be filed in the office of the County Superintendent and be properly preserved for at least one year; and in case any candidate is dissatisfied with the grading of his or her papers, he or she may authorize the County Superintendent to have his or her answers, with the questions, published in any newspaper the examinee may designate.

Pay of com-
mittee.

Time allowed.

Balance fund
how applied.
Ib , Sec. 15.

SEC. 57. It shall be the duty of the County Board to pay the members of the Grading Committee two dollars a day and 5 cents a mile each way, one trip, for the actual distance traveled and for the time necessary to perform their work. In estimating a day, ten hours actual service shall be counted a day, and not more than five days shall be allowed for the completion of the grading of all the papers after any examination. The Grading Committee shall be paid out of the fund created by the examination fees and the balance of said fund shall be kept by the County Board and be applied to employing lecturers and to defraying the expenses of Teachers' Institutes in the county.

TEACHERS' CERTIFICATES.

Who may
teach. Sec. 1,
Chap. 4192.
June 8, 1893.

SECTION 58. No person shall be permitted to teach in the public schools of this State who does not hold a teacher's certificate, granted in accordance with the provisions of this Act.

Five grades of.
Ib., Sec. 2.

SEC. 59. There shall be five grades of certificates issued as herein specified, and named respectively, to-wit: Third Grade, Second Grade, First Grade, State, and Life, Certificates.

Mode of exam-
ination. Ib.,3.

SEC. 60. No certificate, except Life Certificates, shall be issued except on written examination, or written and oral examinations, as provided in this act.

Who eligible.

Fee. Ib. 4.

SEC. 61. Any applicant for a certificate of any grade, before being eligible for examination, shall present to the examiner a written endorsement of good moral character from a responsible person, and shall pay an examination fee of one dollar, which fund shall be applied as hereinafter provided.

Requirements
for Third
Grade. Sec. 1,
Chapter 1331.

SEC. 62. An applicant for a Third Grade Certificate shall be examined in orthography, reading, arithmetic, English grammar, composition, United States history, geography, physiology, and theory and practice of teaching, and must make an average grade in the above-named branches of sixty (60) per cent., with a grade in no branch below forty (40) per cent. The examination in reading shall be both oral and written.

SEC. 63. A Second Grade Certificate shall be issued on examination in the branches as prescribed for Third Grade Certificate. An average grade of seventy-five (75) per cent. shall be required, with a grade in no branch below fifty (50) per cent.

For Second Grade. Ib., Sec. 2.

SEC. 64. An applicant for a First Grade Certificate shall be examined in civil government, algebra and physical geography, in addition to the branches required for a Third Grade Certificate. An applicant for a First Grade Certificate must make an average grade of eighty (80) per cent. and shall grade in no branch below sixty (60) per cent.

For First Grade. Sec. 3.

SEC. 65. A State Certificate shall be issued only by the State Superintendent of Public Instruction to persons holding a First Grade Certificate and who have taught at least twenty-four (24) months, (eight months of which must have been taught in this State successfully under a First Grade Certificate). The Superintendent of Public Instruction shall issue no State Certificate except on written examination in the following branches: Geometry, trigonometry, physics, zoology, botany, Latin, rhetoric, English literature, mental science and general history. A candidate for a State Certificate must make an average grade on the prescribed branches of eighty-five (85) per cent. with the grade in no branch below sixty (60) per cent.

For State Certificate. Ib., Sec. 4.

SEC. 66. Any teacher holding a State Certificate issued under this Act, and such of Chapter 4192 of the Laws of Florida as are not hereby repealed, and who has taught successfully in a High School in this State for the period of thirty (30) months, may be granted a Life Certificate by the State Superintendent, without further examination, if endorsed by three persons holding State Certificates as possessing eminent teaching ability and as having been eminently successful in governing and conducting a school.

For Life Certificate. Ib., Sec. 5.

SEC. 67. Third Grade Certificates shall be good only in the county in which they are issued.

Third Grade limited. Ib., Sec. 7.

SEC. 68. First and Second Grade Certificates may be endorsed by the County Superintendent of any county in the State, and shall then be good in the county in which it is endorsed as well as the one in which it was issued.

First and Second Grades transferrable. Ib., Sec. 8.

SEC. 69. A Third Grade Certificate shall be good for two years from date of issue. A Second Grade Certificate shall be good for three years from date of issue, and a First Grade Certificate shall be good for four years from date of issue.

Term of. Ib., Sec. 10.

And all certificates granted in accordance with the provisions of this act, [Chapter 4331] and such of Chapter 4192 of the laws of Florida as are not hereby repealed, shall be re-issuable upon examination.

Who entitled
to benefits.
Ib., Sec. 12.

SEC. 70. That all persons holding certificates granted in accordance with the provisions of Chapter 4192 of the laws of Florida, shall be entitled to all the benefits and governed by the provisions of this act [*Chap.* 4331].

First Grade issuable upon
what diplomas.

SEC. 71. That any person holding a diploma of graduation from either of the State Normal Colleges of this State, upon presentation of said diploma to any County Superintendent in this State, shall be entitled to a First Grade Certificate without examination; *Provided*, The person holding such diploma applies for such certificate within one year from the granting of such diploma.

Proviso.
Ib., Sec. 13.

Revocation of.
Sec. 18, Chap.
4192.

SEC. 72. A certificate of any grade may be revoked by the authority issuing it, when the holder proves to be unsuccessful, incompetent, or is proven guilty of any gross immorality. A First [or Second] Grade Certificate may be revoked for any of the above reasons by a County Superintendent endorsing it.

DUTIES AND POWERS OF TEACHERS.

SECTION 73. Every teacher is directed—

1st. To labor faithfully and earnestly for the advancement of the pupils in their studies, deportment and morals, and to embrace every opportunity to inculcate, by precept and example, the principles of truth, honesty, patriotism, and the practice of every Christian virtue.

With regards
to studies and
morals.
Rev. Stat.,
Sec. 253.

2d. To require the pupils to observe personal cleanliness, neatness, order, promptness and gentility of manners, to avoid vulgarity and profanity, and to cultivate in them habits of industry and economy, a regard for the rights and feelings of others, and their own responsibilities and duties as citizens.

To habits of
pupils.

School property.

3d. To see that the school-house, and all things pertaining thereto, are not unnecessarily defaced or injured.

To discipline.

4th. To enforce needful restrictions upon the conduct of the pupils in or near the school-house or grounds, avoiding at all times unnecessary severity and measures of punishment that are degrading in their tendency.

To suspend
pupils.

5th. To suspend pupils from school for ten days for gross immorality, misconduct or persistent violations of the regulations, giving immediate notice to the parents or guardian of the pupil, and to the school Supervisor, of the suspension and the cause of it.

6th. To hold a public examination at the close of each school term, either oral or written.

7th. To deliver up the keys and all school property to the Supervisor on closing or suspending the school, and in all things to conform to the regulations of the department.

SEC. 74. No teacher, while actually engaged in his profession, shall be liable to military or jury duty.

SCHOOL SUPERVISORS.

SECTION 75. Every Supervisor is directed—

1st. To supervise the work and management of the school and its interests over which he is appointed, and report monthly to the Board of Public Instruction.

2d. To supervise the construction, rental, repair and improvement of the school buildings, furniture, fences, grounds and fixtures; to procure a copy of the school laws, regulations and decisions for the use of the teacher and for his own instruction.

3d. To attend, at all times, when requested by, and co-operate with the teacher in his efforts to elevate the character and condition of the school; to review all suspensions from school by the teacher of pupils guilty of gross misconduct and a disregard of and persistent opposition to the authority of the teacher, and to promptly report the same to the County Superintendent of Public Instruction.

SEC. 76. Whenever a special school district is created and Trustees are elected, they shall have the supervision of all the public schools within said district. The position of Supervisor shall be suspended by that of Trustees, and the duties prescribed by law for Supervisors shall be performed by the Trustees.

A SCHOOL YEAR, TERM, ETC.

SEC. 77. Beginning with July 1st, A. D. 1898, the school year for all public schools shall begin on the first day of July and end with the last day of the following June; and all reports, financial and otherwise, to the State Department shall embrace such business and matters only as take place within the limits of the school year thus defined.

1899.

When school may begin. Ib., Sec. 2.

SEC. 78. No school in any county shall begin before July 1st of the school year to which that term of school belongs and for which the apportionment was made.

Opening and closing of schools. Ib. Sec. 2.

SEC. 79. The time for the opening of the public schools for each county shall be determined by the County Board of Public Instruction; *Provided*, That all schools must begin so as to close before the last day of June.

School day. Chap 4125, June 8, 1893.

SEC. 80. 1st. A school day shall comprise not less than five (5) and not more than six (6) hours, exclusive of recesses. The time to be fixed by the Board of Public Instruction of each county.

Month.

2d. A school month contains twenty days, exclusive of the first and last days of the week.

Term.

3d. A school term contains four school months.

Year.

4th. The school year contains two terms.

Holidays. Rev Stat., Sec. 256.

SEC. 81. All recognized State or National holidays are school holidays.*

Lost time. Ib., Sec 257.

SEC. 82. Lost time may be made up by a teacher, at the discretion of the School Supervisor, when no conflict would be occasioned with the arrangements of the Board of Public Instruction.

SPECIAL TAX SCHOOLS.

Designation of school districts. Sec. 1. Chapter 4678.

SEC. 83. That each county shall constitute a school unit; that all sub-divisions of a county for school purposes shall be designated as school districts; all school districts levying a school district tax shall hereafter be designated as special tax school districts, and all schools receiving any district tax, as special tax schools.

Election for creating a special tax school district.

SEC. 84. It shall be the duty of the Board of Public Instruction of any county to order an election to be held in any sub-division of any city or incorporated town, community or sub-division of the county, at such time and place as said Board may direct, whenever one-fourth of the qualified electors that pay a tax on real or personal property, and are resident in such city, incorporated town, community, or sub-division of the county, shall petition for such election, to

---

*The legal holidays are: The first day of the week, Sunday, January 1st, New Year's Day; January 19th, Birth Day of Robert E. Lee; February 22d, Washington's Birth-Day; April 26th, Memorial Day; June 3d, Birth-day of Jefferson Davis; July 4th, Independence Day; first Monday in September, Labor Day; General Election Day; Thanksgiving Day; December 25th, Christmas Day.--*Vide* Revised Statutes, Section 2315, and Chapters 4058, 4198, 4817 and 4188, Laws of Florida.

determine whether such city, incorporated town, community or sub-division of the county shall become a special tax school district for the purpose of levying and collecting a district school tax for the exclusive use of public free schools within the district; at such election the following matters shall be determined by a majority of the ballots cast by electors qualified as herein prescribed, except that the three persons receiving the highest vote at such election shall be declared School Trustees of said district: First, whether the city, incorporated town, community or sub-division of the county shall become a special tax school district: Second, who shall be the School Trustees of said district; Third, the number of mills of district tax to be levied and collected annually for the two succeeding years. The three persons receiving the highest number of votes cast shall be declared the Trustees elected for the special tax school district; provided, a majority of all the votes cast be in favor of creating such special tax district, who shall serve for the next ensuing two years and perform the duties hereinafter prescribed.

SEC. 85. The petition mentioned above in this act shall prescribe the boundaries of the sub-division of any city, or city, incorporated town, community or sub-division of the county intended to be formed into a special tax school district. The Board of Public Instruction may, however, change the boundaries thereof before ordering any such election ; but shall in no case include territory not included in original petition, and shall give notice of any such change in the notice of election. Special tax school districts created under this act, shall continue until dis-established or changed by like proceeding as those by which they were created. The petition provided for by Section 2 (Sec. 84) of this act shall be published once a week, for four (4) successive weeks, in some newspaper published in the county having a general circulation throughout the county; and the publication shall state when such petition shall be presented to such Boards. In case there shall be no newspaper published in the county, such petition and notice shall be posted in the manner provided in Section 4 [Sec. 86] of this act for the posting of notice of election.

SEC. 86. It shall be the duty of the Board of Public Instruction of the county to cause a notice of said election to be published once a week for four successive weeks prior thereto in a newspaper published within the county, and having a general circulation throughout the county; but if no newspaper be published in said county, then it shall cause five

1899.

Majority vote necessary.

Matters to be determined.

Term of Trustees. Ib. Sec. 2.

Bounds of district to be prescribed.

Subject to change.

Term of.

Petition to be published. Ib., Sec. 3.

Notice of election to be published.

Who to appoint inspector etc. Ib., Sec. 4.

written or printed notices of said election to be posted in five public places within the territory in which the election is ordered. It shall be the duty of the County Board of Public Instruction to appoint inspectors and clerks for said election, whose duties shall be the same as those of similar officers in general elections, except as herein stated.

Who eligible to vote.

Who pay cost of election. Ib., Sec. 7.

SEC. 87. All qualified voters residing within the territory sought to be made a special tax school district that pay a tax on real or personal property shall be entitled to vote in said election, and a majority of the votes cast shall determine any matter voted upon, pertaining to a special tax school district. The cost of the publication of the notice of such election, and of the election itself, shall be paid by the County Board of Public Instruction out of the first moneys collected from the special tax district.

Mode of conducting elections.

Duty of Supervisor of Registration. Ib., Sec. 6.

SEC. 88. All special tax school district elections shall be held and conducted in the manner prescribed by law for holding general elections, except as provided in this act, and it is hereby made the duty of the Supervisor of Registration of any county to furnish, upon payment for such service, to the County Board of Public Instruction, on demand, a certified list of the qualified voters residing in a special tax school district, or the territory to be created into a special tax school district, that have paid a tax on real or personal property for the year next preceding any such special tax election.

Who to canvass vote. Ib., Sec. 5.

SEC. 89. The Board of Public Instruction shall canvass the returns of election as made to it by the inspectors and clerks of election, and declare the results at the next regular meeting of said Board, or at a special meeting called for that purpose.

Elections to be held biennially. Ib., Sec. 8.

SEC. 90. Elections shall be held bi-ennially in each special tax school district, as near as practicable upon the anniversary of the original election, under the direction of the County Board of Public Instruction, to determine who shall be Trustees for the succeeding two years, and the number of mills of district school tax to be levied for each of said years; said elections shall be held under the same rules and regulations, and qualifications of electors shall be the same as prescribed for those voting in the original election creating a special tax school district.

Form of ballot.

SEC. 91. Each voter voting at any election under this act shall vote but one ballot, and the same shall be written, or printed in black ink on plain white paper, and be substantially

of the following form, according as he may desire to vote upon
any, or all of the questions submitted:

For (or Against) Special Tax School District..............
School Trustees (stating their names)....................

....

....

....

Maximum tax levy .... mills.

Matters to be
vot d on.
1b . sec 17.

Nothing in this act shall have the effect to abrogate
or anywise impair any existing school sub-district, [Spec-
ial Tax School District] but the same are hereafter to be governed by this act.

DUTIES AND POWERS OF SCHOOL TRUSTEES.

Sec. 92. Whenever a special tax school district is created
and Trustees are elected, they shall have the supervision of all
the public schools within said district. The position of Supervisor shall be superseded by that of Trustees, and the duties prescribed by law for Supervisors shall be performed by
the Trustees. The powers of Trustees shall not be those of
control, but of supervision only, and shall extend to all the
public schools within the special district. Any Trustee failing to discharge the duties of the position shall be removed,
after due notice to such Trustee, by the County Board of Public Instruction, and all vacancies occurring in the Board of
Trustees from any cause, shall be filled for the unexpired term
by the County Board of Public Instruction, upon nomination
by the patrons of the school.

To supersede
the Supervisor.

Subject to re-
moval.

Vacancies how
filled. 1b.,
sec. 9.

Sec. 93. All public schools conducted within a special tax
school district shall be under the direction and control of the
County Board of Public Instruction and County Superintendent as in other districts, and subject to the same laws, rules
and regulations prescribed for the conduct of other schools,
except that the Trustees shall have the power to nominate to
the County Board of Public Instruction teachers for all schools
within such special district; *Provided*, That no person be
nominated for teacher who does not hold a teacher's certificate unimpaired by suspension, revocation or limitation, or
that will not remain in full force for the term of school, and
obtained in compliance with the laws of the State. The
County Board of Public Instruction shall have the right to
reject any teacher nominated, and in case the second nomination of a teacher for any position be not ratified, the said

Under control
of County
Board.

May nominate
teachers.

County Board
may reject.
1b.,Sec. 10.

1899.

Board shall then proceed on its own motion, to fill vacancies in the teaching force in any school in the special tax school district.

SEC. 94. The Board of Trustees shall have the further right to say what proportion of the school funds raised within the district shall be applied in any year to buildings, repairs on buildings, to school libraries, to salaries of teachers, and to other educational purposes; *Provided*, That they shall make a fair and equitable distribution of the funds among all the schools in the special tax school district, which shall be shown in their itemized estimate.

To apportion district funds. Ib., sec. 11.

SEC. 95. It shall be the duty of these Trustees, on or before the first day of June in each year, to prepare an itemized estimate, showing the amount of money necessary and likely to be raised for the supplement of the county school funds appropriated to the district for the next ensuing scholastic year, and to certify therein the rate of millage voted to be assessed and collected upon the taxble property within the special tax school district for that year. This estimate shall set forth clearly the apportionment of money raised within the district prorated to each school within the district, stating the amount that will be applied to the salaries of teachers, buildings, furniture or for other educational purposes. It shall also state the number of miles of railroad track and telegraph lines within the bounds of the district. This itemized estimate shall be made in triplicate, one copy to be filed with the Clerk of the Board of County Commissioners, one copy with the Comptroller of the State, one copy with the County Board of Public Instruction; *Provided*, That where there are no railroad or telegraph lines in such district such itemized estimate need not be furnished to the Comptroller. It shall be the duty of the County Commissioners to order the Assessor to assess, and the Collector to collect the amount legally assessed upon the property of the special district, at the rate of millage designated by the Board of Trustees, and pay the same to the County Treasurer; it shall be the duty of the Comptroller of the State to assess all railroads and railroad property, together with telegraph lines and telegraph property situated in such school special district, and to collect the taxes thereon in the same manner as required by law to assess and collect said taxes for State and county purposes, and to remit the same to the Treasurer of the counties, to be by them held to the credit of each special tax school district fund and to be paid out as hereinafter provided. It shall be the duty of the County

To prepare itemized estimate.

To certify millage.

To report railroad and telegraph lines.

With whom to file copies.

Duties of other officers in relation to.

Board of Public Instruction to add the amount set apart for the salaries of teachers in each school within the special tax school district to the county appropriation made for that school, and upon this determine the salaries to be paid teachers and the length of the term that the school shall continue, and contract with teachers for the full term that said fund, arising from both county appropriation and the special tax fund, will sustain the school. The part of this fund arising from the special tax shall be paid to the teachers upon the order of the County Board based upon reports approved by the Trustees, the same as other school funds are paid upon the endorsement of school Supervisors. The County Treasurer shall be liable for all special tax school district funds upon his official bond, after receiving said funds, as in the case of other county revenues.

SEC. 96. The special tax fund set apart by the Board of Trustees for the payment of teachers shall not be subject to requisition for any other purpose by said Trustees; the funds estimated for other educational purposes shall be paid out by warrants of the Board of Public Instruction of the county upon the County Treasurer, said warrants to be based upon requisitions made by the Board of Trustees accompanied by itemized bills for things purchased or work performed. All special funds collected within a school district shall be disbursed solely for school purposes within the district in which collected, and, as near as practicable, in the year in which the tax is collected, upon the recommendation of the Board of Trustees; *Provided*, That the Trustees shall make no contract with one of its members embracing any monetary consideration.

SEC. 97. The Trustees of any school district shall be a corporation and may hold property, sue and be sued, and perform other corporate functions, and perform the usual duties necessary to provide buildings, repair the same, and to purchase libraries and other school appliances; *Provided*, That no debt shall be created without the approval of the County Board of Public Instruction.

SEC. 98. Children residing outside of any special tax school district shall not attend school in any such district without the consent of the Trustees thereof, and of the County Board of Public Instruction; *Provided*, That nothing in this act shall be so construed as to prevent attendance from an adjoining county, provided the County School Board of such ad-

3

1899.

joining county shall pay a pro rata share of such attendance. Such pro rata share to be estimated by the Trustees of such school where such attendance is made; *Provided further*, That pupils from other districts or sub-districts [special tax school districts] shall be subject to same conditions as pupils from other counties as provided in this act.

To audit Tax Collector's Commission. Ext. from Sec. 12, Chap. 4515.

SEC. 99. The commissions for collecting the tax for school sub-districts [special tax school districts] * * shall be audited and allowed by the Trustees of such school, * * and shall be at the rate of two per cent. on such collections.

LAWS RELATING TO POLL TAXES.

SEC. 100. A poll tax of one dollar shall be levied upon each

Duties of Tax Collector in regard to. Sec. 14, Chap. 4322.

male person over the age of twenty-one years, and under the age of fifty-five years, except such as have lost a limb in battle, which tax shall be paid into the county school fund, and shall be collected when taxes on property are collected. It shall be illegal for a Collector to give any receipt for taxes on any property until his poll tax is paid, and the Collector shall on the first day of each month make out a statement giving the names of the parties who have paid their poll taxes, and present the same sworn to by said Collector to the County Commissioners at their regular meeting and present the receipt of the County Treasurer for the same.

Both real and personal property responsible for. Ib., Abbr. Sec. 16.

SEC. 101. * * The assessment of personal property shall be made separate from the assessment of real estate, but personal property shall be responsible for the taxes on real estate, and real estate shall be responsible for the taxes on personal property, and both shall be responsible for a poll tax.

Tax Collector to file certified lists.

SEC. 102. That from and after the passage of this Act it shall be the duty of the Tax Collector in every county of this State to file on or before the tenth day of every month with the County School Board [County Board of Public Instruction], a certified list of the names of all persons whose poll taxes were paid during the previous month, giving the year for which such payments were made. A copy of this list shall also be filed with the County Commissioners with a receipt from the County Treasurer for the amount collected as such poll taxes. It shall be the duty of the School

School Board to examine his books.

Board [County Board of Public Instruction] to examine at least twice each year the books and records of the Tax Collector which relate to the collection of poll taxes and said Board shall require prompt settlement for all poll taxes assessed, together with those not assessed but collected.

Any Tax Collector or member of a County School Board [County Board of Public Instruction] who shall neglect to comply with the provisions of this act shall be suspended from office.

SEC. 103. It shall be the duty of the County Superintendent of Public Instruction, acting as Secretary of the County School Board [County Board of Public Instruction], to make and forward monthly a certified copy of the monthly lists of persons who have paid their poll taxes, mentioned in Section 1 [Sec. 102] of this Act, to the State Superintendent of Public Instruction, who shall file and preserve the same in his office as a part of the public records and furnish copies thereof when requested by citizens of this State.

DUTIES OF OFFICERS IN REGARD TO SCHOOL TAXES AND FUNDS.

SEC. 104. It shall be the duty of the Assessor in each county, immediately after the assessment of the county has been reviewed and equalized by the County Commissioners, and the amount to be raised for State and county and school sub-district [special tax school district] and road sub-district purposes determined, to calculate and carry out the total amount of State taxes and the total amount of county taxes, and the total amount of school sub-district [special tax school district] and road sub-district taxes in three separate columns prepared for that purpose in the assessment roll, setting opposite to the aggregate sum set down as the valuation of real and personal estate the respective sums assessed as taxes thereon in dollars and cents, etc.

SEC. 105. The County Commissioners shall determine the amount to be raised for all county purposes, and shall enter upon their minutes the rate to be levied for each fund respectively, and shall ascertain the aggregate rate necessary to cover all such taxes and report the same to the Assessor, who shall carry out the full amount of taxes for all county purposes under one heading in the assessment roll to be provided for that purpose, and the County Commissioners shall notify the Clerk and Auditor of the county, also the Treasurer thereof, of the amount to be apportioned to the different accounts out of the total taxes levied for all purposes, and the County Treasurer in issuing receipts to the Collector shall state in each of his receipts, which shall be in duplicate, the amount apportioned to each fund out of the payment made to him by the Collector, and when any such receipts shall be given to the Collector by the County Treasurer, he shall immediately file one of the same with the Clerk and Auditor of the county who shall credit the same to the Collector with the amoun thereof, and shall make out and deliver to the Collector a cert tificate setting forth the payment in detail, as shown by the Treasurer's receipt; *Provided*, That the Trustees of each school sub-district [special tax school district] and road sub-district shall file a written statement with the Tax Assessor setting forth the boundary of such school sub-district [special tax school district] and road sub-district, and the rate of tax-ation to be levied on the real and personal property therein as provided by law, and the Assessor shall, upon receipt of such statement, proceed to assess such property and enter the taxes thereon in separate columns in the assessment roll to be provided for that purpose.

SEC. 106. To the assessment roll for 1897 and subsequent years, delivered to the Tax Collector, a warrant under the hand of the Assessor shall be annexed in the following form, to-wit:

State of Florida, to..............., Tax Collector of the county of.........................: You are hereby commanded to collect out of the real estate and per-sonal property, and from each of the persons and corporations named in the annexed roll, the taxes set down in each roll opposite each name, corporation or parcel of land therein described, and in case the taxes so imposed are not paid at the time prescribed by law, you are to collect the same by levy and sale of the goods and chattels, lands and tenements so assessed, or of the person or corporation so taxed; and all sums collected for State taxes, you are to pay to the State Treasurer at such time as may be required by law, and at the same time you are to pay to the County Treasurer all sums collected for county taxes, and to the Treasurer of the County Board of Public Instruction all sums collected for school taxes, and at the same time you are to pay to the duly qualified Trus-tees [to the County Treasurer—See Sec. 12, Chapter 4678] of each school sub-district [special tax school district] and road sub-district all sums collected for school sub-district [special tax school] and road sub-district taxes, and you are further required to make all collections on or before the first Monday in April; and on or before the first Monday in July, you will make a final report to and settlement with the Comptroller and County Commissioners.

Given under my hand and seal, this the.................

.........day of...............in the year A. D. 189....

...................., Assessor of.............County.

Sec. 107. As soon as the assessment roll shall be delivered to the Collector, the Clerk of the Circuit Court shall make out and publish a statement showing the amount of taxes charged to the Collector to be collected for the current year and the apportionment of the same in separate columns to the several funds for which such taxes have been levied, including all poll taxes, which poll taxes shall be itemized separately in all state- ments both as to amounts assessed and as to the amounts col- lected, and at each monthly meeting of the County Commis- sioners thereafter, and until the tax books are closed, he shall publish a statement giving each fund credit with the amount collected thereon as shown by the reports of the Tax Collec- tor in his office, and when the tax books are closed he shall publish a like statement showing the amounts specifically al- lowed the collector on account of errors and insolvencies, and the amount of each fund uncollected. The aforesaid state- ments shall be posted by the Clerk at the court house door, and published in a newspaper when one is published in the county, and the costs of publishing the same shall be paid by the County Commissioners. Any Clerk failing to publish such statements shall be guilty of a misdemeanor, and upon convic- tion be punished by a fine not exceeding two hundred dollars, or by imprisonment not exceeding one year; and it shall be the duty of the Circuit Court Judges to charge this section to the grand juries in their respective counties.

Duty of Clerk of Court to ap- portion and publish amount of each tax.

polls to be itemized sep- arately.

Publish col- lections monthly.

Penalty for failure.

Duty of Circuit Judges. Sec. 34, Chap. 4322, June 1, 1895.

Sec. 108. * * The County Commissioners of each county shall levy a tax not to exceed five mills nor less than three and one-quarter (3¼) mills on the dollar on the real and personal property of the county for school purposes.

Duty of County Com- missioners. Ext. Sec. 2, Chap. 4516.

Note.—Fixing the minimum county levy for schools at 3¼ mills is undoubtedly unconstitutional.

Sec. 109. * * Orders upon the County Treasurer of any county shall be receivable by such county for county revenue, and orders issued by the County Board of Public Instruction shall be receivable in the counties where such orders are issued for county school taxes.

County orders receivable for taxes. Ib., Ext. Sec. 39.

Sec. 110. No collector of any county shall either directly or indirectly purchase or receive in exchange any Comptroller's warrants, county orders, jurors' certificates, or school district orders, for a less amount than expressed on the face of such orders or demand, any such person so offending shall for each

Penalty for Tax Collector dealing in state or County securities. Ib., Sec. 40.

1899.

offense be deemed guilty of a misdemeanor, and, on conviction thereof, shall be fined in the sum of not less than one thousand dollars, nor more than ten thousand dollars, and be removed from office.

SEC. 111. The Treasurer of the [State] Board of Education shall keep an account with the several counties, in which he shall credit each county with its proportion of the income of the common school fund, and of the fund raised by the one mill tax authorized by the Constitution, and shall charge each with the amounts receipted for by the Treasurers of the Boards of Public Instruction.

Duty of State
Treasurer.
Rev. Stat.,
Sec. 262.

SEC. 112. Every officer having moneys which by law go to the State school fund shall pay the same to the State Treasurer, and every officer having moneys which by law go to the county school fund shall pay the same to the County Treasurer.

To whom pay
School funds.
Ib., Sec. 264.

SEC. 113. It shall be the duty of the Treasurer of the school fund of each county in this State by the first Monday in each and every month, to prepare and file with the County Superintendent of Public Instruction of his county a detailed and itemized statement in writing, showing all sums of money received by such Treasurer during the month next preceding, and from whom and from what source received, and all amounts by him paid out during such time and to whom paid, and describing by date, number and amount all warrants paid.

Duty of County Treasurer to make monthly reports.
Sec. 1, Chapter 1332.

SEC. 114. The financial statements of account [Sec. 40, Pars. 9th and 10th] hereinbefore provided for, when filed with the Clerk of the Circuit Court, shall be securely kept by him and shall at all times be open to the examination and inspection of the people of the county without fee or charge.

Duty of clerk of Court to preserve reports.
Ib., Sec. 4.

SEC. 115. The County Treasurer shall enter in a book to be kept by him for that purpose, the fact of the refusal to pay, or non-payment of any warrant which may be presented to him, as such treasurer, and include in such entry a description of the warrant or order, and by whom presented, and date of presentation, and his reason for such refusal or non-payment; and he shall also, at the request of the person presenting the same, endorse on the back of such warrant the fact of such refusal or non-payment and reason therefor, and shall pay such warrants in the order of their presentation. The Board of County Commissioners of each county shall furnish the Treasurer a book for the purpose above specified, which shall be open to the inspection of all citizens.

Duty of County Treasurer to keep description of warrants not paid.

To pay them in order of presentation.
Sec. 1, Chap. 4409.

COUNTY BOARDS OF PUBLIC INSTRUCTIONS MAY CONTRACT DEBTS OR BORROW MONEY.

SEC. 116. That the Board of County Commissioners upon the request of the Board of Public Instruction after an affirmative vote of the qualified voters who are tax-payers therein and have paid all taxes due by them for two years next and preceding said election in any sub-school [special tax school] district or county which debt shall be a charge or lien only upon such sub-school district [special tax school district] or county as the case may be, are hereby authorized to contract debts for the purchase of real estate to be used for educational purposes, for the erection of school buildings, and to pay such debts out of the current income of any year, or out of the income of succeeding years: *Provided*, That the necessary expense of maintaining the schools in any county during any year shall constitute the first claim against the school fund of that year.

Vote of certain electors required, etc.

School expenses first claim on school fund. See 1, Chapter 4682.

SEC. 117. That the Board of County Commissioners upon the request of the Board of Public Instruction after an affirmative vote of the qualified voters who are tax-payers therein and have paid all taxes due by them for two years next and preceding said election in any sub-school district [special tax school district] or county, which debt shall be a charge or lien only upon such sub-school district or county as the case may be, are hereby authorized to borrow money from time to time as occasion may require to discharge any debt or liability incurred for the purchase of real estate for educational purposes, for the erection of school buildings, and to pay the interest and principal out of the current income of any year, or out of the income of succeeding years; *Provided*, That the necessary expense of maintaining the schools in any county during any year shall constitute the first claim against the school fund of that year.

How may borrow money.

School expenses constitute first claim in any year. Ib., Sec. 2.

COUNTY LINE PUPILS.

SEC. 118. When it is more convenient for youth residing in one county to attend school in an adjoining county, they may do so by the concurrence of the Superintendents of Public Instruction of the two counties. The proportion of school money for each youth shall be transferred by requisition of the County Superintendent of Public Instruction of the county in which the youth resides, upon the Treasurer of the school funds of that county to the Treasurer of the school funds of the county in which the school is located.

When permitted to go to school in another county.

Funds how transferred. Rev. Stat., Sec. 258.

SCHOOL FUNDS. WHEN FORFEITED.

When a county forfeits.
Rev. Stat.,
Sec. 259.

SEC. 119. Any county or school district neglecting to establish an maintain such school or schools as the available funds will support, shall forfeit its proportion of the common school fund during such neglect, and in that case all moneys so forfeited shall be apportioned among the several counties at the next annual apportionment.

When a school forfeits
Sec. 3. Chap.
4196, June 2.
1893.

SEC. 120. Any public school in the county failing to complete its public term before the terminus of the school year shall forfeit the proportion of its financial apportionment not used by neglecting or failing to maintain a school for the full term of school in that county, and in that case all moneys so forfeited shall be apportioned among the several schools of the county at the next annual apportionment.

PENALTIES.

For insulting teacher.
Rev. Stat.,
Sec. 2623.

SEC. 121. Whoever, within the school house or grounds, upbraids or insults any teacher in the presence of the pupils, shall be punished by imprisonment not exceeding fifteen days, or by fine not exceeding twenty-five dollars. This section shall not apply to any pupil in and subject to the discipline of the school.

For disturbing a school.
Ib., Sec. 2629.

SEC. 122. Whoever willfully interrupts or disturbs any school * * shall be punished by imprisonment not exceeding thirty days, or by fine not exceeding fifty dollars.

For introducing obscene prints and literature into.
Ib., Sec. 2620.

SEC. 123. Whoever imports, prints, publishes, sells or distributes any book, pamphlet, ballad, printed paper or other things containing obscene language, or any obscene prints, figures, pictures or descriptions manifestly tending to the corruption of the morals of youth, or introduces into any * * school or place of education, or buys, procures, receives, or has in his possession any such book, pamphlet, ballad, printed paper or other thing, either for the purpose of sale, exhibition, loan or circulation or with the intent to introduce the same into any * * school, or place of education, shall be punished by imprisonment in the State prison not exceeding five years, or in the county jail not exceeding one year, or by fine not exceeding one hundred dollars.

For obscenity on school buildings
Ib., Sec. 2621

SEC. 124. Whoever willfully cuts, paints, pastes or defaces by writing or in any other manner any school building, furniture, apparatus, appliance, outbuilding, ground, fence, tree, post or other school property, with obscene word, image or device, shall be punished by imprisonment not exceeding fifteen days, or by fine not exceeding one hundred dollars. This section shall not apply to any pupil in and subject to the discipline of the school.

SEC. 125. Whoever willfully and maliciously, or wantonly and without cause, destroys, defaces, mars or injures * * any school house, * * or other building erected or used for the purpose of education, * * or for the general diffusion of knowledge, or any of the outbuildings, fences, walls, or appurtenances of such school house, * * or other building, or any furniture, apparatus or other property belonging to or connected with such school house, * * or other building, shall be punished by imprisonment not exceeding one year, or by fine not exceeding five hundred dollars.

For injuring school houses. Ib., Sec. 2531.

SEC. 126. No Superintendent or School Board of any county, or any person officially connected with the government or direction of the public schools, or teacher thereof, shall receive any private fee, gratuity, donation or compensation, in any manner whatsoever, for promoting the sale or the exchange of any school book, map or chart in any public school, or be an agent for the sale, or the publisher of any school text-book, or be directly or indirectly pecuniarily interested in the introduction of any such text-book; and any such agency or interest shall disqualify any person so acting or interested from holding any school office whatsoever, and shall be deemed a misdemeanor, and upon conviction the party so offending shall be fined in a sum not exceeding fifty dollars, or imprisoned not less than thirty days.

For school officers being interested in sale &c., of text-books.

To be debarred from holding office. Ib., Sec. 266.

SEC. 127. Any Superintendent or School Board of any county, or any person officially connected with the government or direction of a public school, or teacher thereof, who violates the provisions of Section 7 [126 above], shall be punished by imprisonment not exceeding thirty days, or by fine not exceeding fifty dollars.

To be imprisoned or fined. Ib., 2736.

SEC. 128. Any Superintendent, county or State, violating the provisions of this Act, [Chapter 4192, concerning examination and certification of teachers] upon conviction shall be fined not less that fifty nor more than one hundred dollars, and shall be debarred from holding any school office in this State.

For violating laws examination. Sec. 21, Chap, 4192.

SEC. 129. Members of Boards of Publi Instruction, County Superintendents of Public Instruction and Treasurers of county school funds, who shall fail or cause to perform any of the duties required of them by the provisions of this Act,

For failing to mak lish Sec, 433

1899.

[Chapter 4332, concerning making and publishing reports] shall for such neglect of duty be subject and liable to suspension and removal from office by the Governor, under the provisions of Section 15, of Article IV, of the Constitution.

EAST AND WEST FLORIDA SEMINARIES.

SEC. 130. Each county in this State east or west of the Suwannee river shall be entitled to send to said Seminary in the division in which such county is located, as many scholars or beneficiaries as it may have Representatives in the House of Representatives of Florida, who shall receive all the benefits of instruction of said Seminary free of all charge.

Beneficiary scholars. R. S., Sec. 311.

SEC. 131. At least once in each year each Seminary shall be visited by three suitable persons—not members of the Board or Seminary—to be appointed by the Board [of Trustees], who shall examine thoroughly into the affairs of the Seminary, and report to the State Superintendent of Public Instruction their views with regard to its condition, success and usefulness, and any other matters they may judge expedient. Such visitors shall be appointed annually.

Board of Visitors.

To report. Ib., Sec. 312.

FLORIDA NORMAL SCHOOL AND BUSINESS INSTITUTE.

SEC. 132. * * One white student, male or female, from each Senatorial District in the State shall be admitted to all the rights and privileges of the Literary and Classical Departments of the * * Florida Normall School and Business Institute, free of tuition; *Provided*, That appointments to scholarships to the Florida Normal School and Business Institute shall be made by Senators of the various Senatorial Districts of the State of Florida.

Students admitted free of tuition. Abbr. Sec. 2. Chap. 3869. May 30, 1889.

AGRICULTURAL COLLEGE.

SEC. 133. * * Each county shall be entitled to send annually, or so often as vacancies may occur, one student for each member of the Assembly from that county; such student shall be selected by the Boards of Public Instruction of the several counties from among the most advanced pupils in the common and higher schools therein who may present themselves as candidates. Each County Board of Public Instruction shall annually, or as often as vacancies occur which should be filled by the county, give early notice of such vacancy, and of the time and place of meeting for the examination of the candidates. The County Board shall then and there, by

Each county entitled to one student for each member of the Assembly.

themselves, or with the assistance of such persons as they may appoint, examine said candidates, and select those best qualified as to scholastic attainments, good health and upright moral character, and furnish them with certificates of selection for admission, subject to the re-examination and approval of the faculty of the college. In case any [County] Board of Instruction fails to attend to the above duty, then pupils holding high rank in their schools in that county may make application in person to the faculty of the college and be examined and admitted on the same terms as they would have been had they passed a preliminary examination before the [County] Board of Instruction of their county. But in case such vacancies remained unfilled, students may be selected from the State at large by the faculty.

Selected by the County Board of Public Instruction by examination.

May make application to the Faculty. Abbr. Sec. 291. R. S.

SEC. 134. Each Senator, during his term of office, shall be empowered to nominate one student, who shall be a resident of his Senatorial District, to said State Agricultural College, who shall be entitled to receive the benefit of a full course of instruction at said college without any charge for tuition, subject to such rules and regulations as may be established for the government and direction of said college.*

State Senators to nominate one student. Ib., Sec. 295.

SEC. 135. The trustees shall make an annual report to the Superintendent of Public Instruction on or before the first day of October, to be by him printed with his report and laid before the Legislature at the beginning of each regular session. Such report shall give a full exposition of the financial condition of the corporation, the progress and improvements made, the nature, cost and results of experiments, and such other matters, including State industrial and economical statistics, as may be supposed useful; one copy of which the Superintendent shall transmit by mail to each of the other colleges which were endowed under the provisions of the act of Congress of July 2, 1862; also a copy to the Secretary of the Interior, and one to each house of Congress.

Trustees to report to Superintendent of Public Instruction. Ib., Sec. 297.

NOTE.--The College now admits all who apply free of tuition.

APPENDIX.

Some of The Session Laws of 1893.

CHAPTER 4192.

AN ACT to Prescribe Rules and Regulations for Licensing Teachers; to Provide for Uniform Examinations; to Secure Fairness in Examinations and in Issuing Teachers' Certificates, and for Other Purposes.

Be it enacted by the Legislature of the State of Florida:

SECTION 1. No person shall be permitted to teach in the public schools of the State who does not hold a teacher's certificate, granted in accordance with the provisions of this Act. *(Who to teach schools.)*

SEC. 2. There shall be five grades of certificates issued as herein specified, and named respectively, to-wit: Third grade, second grade, first grade, State, and life, certificates. *(Certificates, how graded.)*

SEC. 3. No certificate, except life certificates, shall be issued, except on written examination, or written and oral examinations, as provided in this Act.

SEC. 4. Any applicant for a certificate of any grade, before being eligible for examination, shall present to the examiner a written endorsement of good moral character from a responsible person, and shall pay an examination fee of one dollar, which fund shall be applied as hereinafter provided. *(Good character.)*

SEC. 5. An applicant for a third grade certificate shall be examined in orthography, reading, arithmetic, English grammar, composition, penmanship, United States history, geography, physiology, and theory and practice of teaching, and must make an average grade on the above named branches of sixty (60) per cent., with a grade in no branch below forty (40) per cent. The examination in reading shall be both oral and written. A third grade certificate shall be good for the period of one year from date of issue, and no person shall be permitted to teach longer than one year under a third grade certificate. *(Qualifications for third Grade Certificates.)*

1899.

For Second Grade.

SEC. 6. A second grade certificate shall be issued on examination in the branches as prescribed for a third grade certificate. An average grade of seventy-five (75) per cent., shall be required, with the grade in no branch below ·fifty (50) per cent., which certificate shall be good two years from date of issue. No teacher shall be granted more than two second grade certificates.

For First Grade.

SEC. 7. An applicant for a first grade certificate shall be examined in civil government, book-keeping, algebra, and physical geography, in addition to the branches required for a third grade certificate. An appellant for a first grade certificate must make an average grade of eighty (80) per cent., and shall grade in no branch below sixty (60) per cent. A first grade certificate shall be good for three years from date of its issue.

State Certificates, how issued.

SEC. 8. A State certificate shall be issued only by the State Superintendent of Public Instruction to persons holding a first grade certificate and who have taught at least twenty-four (24) months (eight months of which must have been taught in this State successfully under a first grade certificate). The Superintendent of Public Instruction shall issue no State certificate, except on written examination in the following branches in addition to those required for a first grade certificate: Geometry, trigonometry, physics, zoology, botany, Latin, rhetoric, English literature, mental science and general history.

Average Grade.

A candidate for State certificate must make an average grade on the prescribed branches of eighty-five (85) per cent., with the grade in no branch below sixty (60) per cent. A State certificate shall be good for five years from date of issue.

Life Certificates, who entitled to.

SEC. 9. Any teacher holding a State certificate issued under this Act, and who has taught successfully in a high school in this State for the period of thirty (30) months, may be granted a life certificate by the State Superintendent, without further examination, if endorsed by three persons holding State certificates as possessing eminent teaching ability and as having been eminently successfully in governing and conducting a school. Nothing in this Act shall prevent the State Superintendent from granting special life certificates to eminently successful kindergarten or primary teachers, who have taught three years in this State, good only in that department of schools.

Mode of examination.

SEC. 10. Candidates for third, second, or first grade certificates shall be examined by the County Superintendent of Public Instruction on questions prepared in all cases by the

State Superintendent of Public Instruction. The questions shall be sent sealed to the County Superintendents of the various counties, which seals shall not be broken until the morning of the day on which the questions for that day are to be used, and then only in the presence of the persons assembled for examination. Any person or persons who shall be found guilty of securing or attempting to secure the prepared questions, or who shall furnish the prepared questions to any teacher or other person in any other way than prescribed by this Act, shall be debarred from teaching a school or from holding any school office in this State. The candidates for certificates shall ask no questions, nor receive assistance from any source during the examination. In case any examinee may be in doubt as to the meaning of any question, he or she may state in writing the point in doubt and answer accordingly, which answer shall receive due consideration in grading the papers.

SEC. 11. All examination papers shall be prepared in the presence of the County Superintendent or his appointed assistant, who shall collect the questions and answers on each branch as completed, and said examiner shall accept no paper of any examinee containing a name or mark which would indicate to any other than the examiner its author. Said examiner shall himself, on collecting each paper, designate it by a number known only to himself, and shall keep a record by number and by name of the author of each examination paper. Every examinee shall complete and hand in the answers on each branch before the questions on any other branch shall be given out. When every examinee has completed all the branches, the examiner shall arrange and bundle together all the papers of each examinee, and shall deliver the whole to a grading committee.

Who to prepare examination papers.

SEC. 12. The County Board of Public Instruction, prior to any authorized examination, shall appoint three teachers holding the highest grade certificates among the teachers of the county as a grading committee; said committee shall, immediately after the close of any examination, carefully examine and grade, agreeably to instructions sent out by the State Superintendent, each paper turned over to it by the County Superintendent. When the said committee shall have completed its work it shall deliver back to the County Superintendent all papers turned over to it, with a gradation sheet showing the shade of each examinee in each branch upon which he or she was examined, also the average grade and rank of each examinee. The County Superintendent shall

Grading Committee.

Duties of such Committee.

1899.

then, for the first time, make known to the grading committee the name corresponding to the number of any examinee, and shall then in the presence of said committee present his list and write on said gradation sheet the name of each examinee after his or her proper number. The said grading committee shall retain one copy of said gradation sheet and shall file one with the County Superintendent, who shall issue certificates to the examinees making averages according to the provisions of Sections 5, 6 and 7 of this Act, and to no others.

Where exami- nation papers to be filed.

SEC. 13. All examination questions and answers prepared by the applicants for certificates shall be filed in the office of the County Superintendent and properly preserved for at least one year, and in case any candidate is dissatisfied with the grading of his or her papers, he or she may authorize the County Superintendent to have his or her answers, with the questions, published in any newspaper the examinee may designate.

To keep secret names of Com- mittee.

SEC. 14. It shall be the duty of the County Board of Pub- lic Instruction, before every public examination, to appoint a grading committee, and to keep secret the names of persons comprising said committee until its work is performed.

Fees.

SEC. 15. It shall be the duty of the County Board to pay the members of the grading committee two dollars a day and five cents a mile each way one trip for the actual distance traveled and for the time necessary to perform their work. In estimating a day, ten hours' actual service shall be counted a day, and not more than five days shall be allowed for the com- pletion of the grading of all the papers after any examination. The grading committee shall be paid out of the fund created by the examination fees, and the balance of said funds shall be kept by the County Board and be applied to employing lec- turers and to defraying the expenses of Teachers' Institutes in the county.

Extent of Cer- tificates.

SEC. 16. Third and second grade certificates shall be good only in the county in which they are issued.

First Grade Certificates to be endorsed.

SEC. 17. Any first grade certificate may be endorsed by the County Superintendent of any county in the State, and then will become good for its unexpired time in the county in which it is endorsed, as well as in the one in which it was issued. State and life certificates granted in accordance with this Act shall be good throughout the State for the periods for which they are granted.

Revocation of Certificate.

SEC. 18. A certificate of any grade may be revoked by the authority issuing it, when the holder proves to be unsuccessful, incompetent, or is proven guilty of any gross immorality. A first grade certificate may be revoked for any of the above reasons by a County Superintendent endorsing it.

SEC. 19. There shall be held two examinations a year in each county in the State, beginning on Tuesday after the first Monday in May and September, and each may continue one or more days at the discretion of the examiner and a vote of the examinees; *Provided*, That only one examination may be held in any county, if two be found unnecessary.

Two examinations.

SEC. 20. The State Superintendent, for sufficient cause, may order examinations held on days other than those prescribed by Section 19 of this Act.

When to be held.

SEE. 21. Any Superintendent, county or State, violating the provisions of this act, upon conviction shall be fined not less than fifty nor more than one hundred dollars, and shall be debarred from holding any school office in this State.

Penalty.

SEC. 22. All laws and parts of laws in conflict with this Act are hereby repealed.

Repeal.

SEC. 23. This Act shall take effect after January 1st, 1894.

Approved June 8, 1893.

CHAPTER 4193.

AN ACT to Provide for the Election of Members of County Boards of Public Instruction, and to Fix their Compensation.

Be it Enacted by the Legislature of the State of Florida:

SECTION 1. That at the next general election, and every two years thereafter, there shall be elected in each county in this State a County Board of Public Instruction, hereinafter mentioned as the County School Board, consisting of three members, whose terms of office shall begin the first Tuesday after the first Monday in January after such election, and terminate upon the qualification of their successors two years thereafter.

Election of County School Boards.

SEC. 2. At the first meeting in July, 1894, the County Board of Public Instruction in each county shall divide their respective counties into three county school board districts so as to place in each district, as nearly as practicable, the same number of qualified voters, the lines of said districts being so drawn as to place each election district wholly within one or another of said county school board districts; and the members of the County School Board shall file in the office of the Clerk of the Circuit Court for such county a certificate of

Duties of County Boards of Public Instruction.

4

1899.

their said action, containing a description of the boundaries of said districts, and naming the election districts comprising each county school board district, which certificate shall be published in a newspaper published in the county, or if there be no newspaper published in the county, then by posting at the county court house door for four weeks thereafter. The County School Board may thereafter change the boundaries of any such districts at a meeting in July of the year of a general election, but such change shall be certified in the Clerk's office and published as required for fixing such districts in the first instance.

Boundaries of Districts.

SEC. 3. The members of the County School Board shall be elected one from each county school board district by the qualified electors of such district.

Election by School Districts.

SEC. 4. All vacancies on said Board shall be filled for the unexpired term by appointment by the State Board of Education on the nomination of the State Superintendent of Public Instruction.

Filling vacancies.

SEC. 5. The members of the County School Board shall be paid from the county school fund for their services, two dollars per day for each day's service, and not exceeding five cents per mile for traveling expenses. All traveling expenses, before being paid, shall be itemized and approved by the Board.

Fees.

SEC. 6. All laws and parts of laws in conflict herewith are hereby repealed in so far as they conflict with this Act.

Repeal.

Approved June 2. 1893.

CHAPTER 4194.

AN ACT to Provide for School Sub-Districts in Counties and Towns, and to Provide for the Levying and Collection of Taxes for the Support of Schools in such Sub-Districts.

Be it Enacted by the Legislature of the State of Florida:

SECTION 1. That an election may be held under the order and direction of the Board of Public Instruction of any county, if they shall deem it advisable, in any election district, or incorporated city or town of such county, upon the petition of one-fourth of the registered and qualified voters thereof, who are taxpayers on real or personal property therein, and have paid all taxes due by them for two years next preceding the presentation of such petition, to determine whether such election district, city or town, shall be a school sub-district. Any

Election to form School Sub-Districts.

such election shall be held, and the result ascertained and declared as nearly as practicable in the same manner, as is provided by law for the holding of elections concerning Article XIX of the Constitution, substituting the Board of Public Instruction for the County Commissioners. It shall require a majority of the votes of those voting at any such election to determine any matter in the affirmative. If such sub-district is created, three school trustees shall be elected therein, upon a day to be fixed by the Board of ·Public Instruction, and on the same day bi-ennially thereafter.

Mode of election.

Sec. 2. All voters in such election for sub-districts or trustees shall have the qualifications specified in section one for petitioners for elections to establish sub-districts.

Qualifications for voters.

Sec. 3. It shall be the duty of these trustees, on or before the last Monday in June of each year, to prepare an itemized estimate, showing the amount of money required for the necessary common school purposes of their sub-district for the next ensuing scholastic year; stating the rate of millage to be assessed and collected upon the taxable property of their sub-district to cover such amount, not to exceed three mills on the dollar. A copy of the itemized estimate herein provided for shall be filed with the Clerk of the Board of County Commissioners, which Board shall direct the Assessor of Taxes to assess, and the Collector to collect the amount so stated. Moneys collected under provisions of this Act shall be paid over to the trustees of the sub-districts in which the tax is levied.

Duty of Trustees.

Sec. 4. These trustees shall, under the direction of the Board of Public Instruction, supervise each school in their district, and see that the teachers perform their work promptly and energetically, and that the general work, discipline and moral of the school is satisfactory, and report to the Board of Public Instruction at their regular monthly meetings.

Further duties of Trustees.

Sec. 5. They shall also be a corporation with the usual powers for the purpose of performing their duties.

To be corporate.

Sec. 6. They shall receive and hold the money which may be assessed and collected as hereinbefore provided, as a special tax to be disbursed in the district where collected solely for school purposes, such as building school houses, furnishing the same, repairing, heating and cleansing, and when necessary paying any legitimate deficit due the teachers. These trustees shall be required to give bond in twice the amount raised by the special tax, to be approved by the County Board of Public Instruction before receiving any such money.

Powers.

1899.

Mode of abol-
ishing.

SEC. 7. Any sub-district may be abolished by like proceedings as those above provided for its establishment. The boundaries of such sub-district shall coincide with the boundaries of the election district, excepting that if a portion of an election district being in an incorporated city or town shall be included in a sub-district composed of such city or town, the remainder of such election district not included in such city or town may become a school sub-district in the same manner as though it were an entire election district.

Repeal.

SEC. 8. That all laws and parts of laws in conflict with this Act be and the same are hereby repealed.

SEC. 9. That this Act shall take effect from and after its passage and approval by the Governor.

Approved June 2, 1893.

CHAPTER 4195.

AN ACT to Amend Section 255 of the Revised Statutes of the State of.Florida, and to Define and Declare What Number of Hours Shall Comprise a School Day.

Be it Enacted by the Legislature of the State of Florida:

SECTION 1. That Section 255, Revised Statutes of the State of Florida, be amended so as to read as follows:

What to con-
stitute school
day.

255. SCHOOL DAY, MONTH, TERM AND YEAR.—First. A school day shall comprise not less than five (5) and not more than six (6) hours, exclusive of recesses. The time to be fixed by the Board of Public Instruction of each county. Second. A school month contains twenty days, exclusive of the first and last days of the week. Third. A school term contains four school months. Fourth. A school year contains two terms.

Approved June 6, 1893.

CHAPTER 4196.

AN ACT to Define a School Year, and to Provide for the Opening and Closing of School Terms.

Be it Enacted by the Legislature of the State of Florida:

Beginning of
school year.

SECTION 1. That, beginning with July 1st, A. D. 1893, the school year for all public schools shall begin on the first day of July and end with the last day of the following June; and that all reports, financial and otherwise, to the State Department shall embrace such business and matters only as take place within the limits of the school year thus defined.

SEC. 2. The time for the opening of the public schools for each county shall be determined by the County Board of Public Instruction; *Provided*, That all schools must begin so as to close before the last day of June.

Time of opening schools.

SEC. 3. Any public school in the county failing to complete its public term before the terminus of the school year, shall forfeit the proportion of its financial apportionment not used by neglecting or failing to maintain a school for the full term of school in that county, and in that case all moneys so forfeited shall be apportioned among the several schools of the county at the next annual apportionment.

Forfeit of. moneys.

SEC. 4. No school in any county shall begin before July first of the school year to which that term of school belongs and for which the apportionment is made.

No school to begin before July 1st.

SEC. 5. All laws and parts of laws in conflict with this Act are hereby repealed.

Approved June 2, 1893.

RESOLUTION No. 3.

HOUSE JOINT RESOLUTION Proposing an Amendment to the Constitution of the State of Florida.

Be it Resolved by the Legislature of the State of Florida:

That the following amendment to the Constitution of the State of Florida be, and the same is hereby agreed to, and shall be submitted to the electors of the State at the general election in October, A. D. 1994, for ratification or rejection:

Amendment. to Sec. 7, Art. XII, of the Constitution.

Section 7, of Article 12, of the Constitution is hereby amended so as to read as follows:

SECTION 7. Provision shall be made by law for the apportionment and distribution of the interest on the State School Fund and all other means provided, including the special tax for the support and maintenance of public free schools, among the several counties of the State in proportion to the average attendance upon schools in the said counties respectively.

Apportionment of School Fund.

Approved June 2, 1893.

CHAPTER 4331—[No. 10.]

AN ACT to Amend Sections 5, 6, 7, 8, 9, 12, 16, 17 and 19, of Chapter 4192, of the Laws of Florida, the same being "An Act Entitled an Act to Prescribe Rules and Regulations for Licensing Teachers, to Provide for Uniform Examinations; to Secure Fairness in Examinations and in Issuing Teachers' Certificates and for Other Purposes."

Be it Enacted by the Legislature of the State of Florida:

SECTION 1. That Section 5, of Chapter 4192, of the Laws of Florida be, and the same is hereby amended to read as follows:
An applicant for a third grade certificate shall be examined in orthography, reading, arithmetic, English grammer, composition, United States history, geography, physiology and theory and practice of teaching, and must make an average grade in the above named branches of sixty (60) per cent. with a grade in no branch below forty (40) per cent. The examination in reading shall be both oral and written.

Applicant for Third Grade Certificate.

SEC. 2. That Section 6, of Chapter 4192, of the Laws of Florida be, and the same is hereby amended to read as follows: A second grade certificate shall be issued on examination in the branches as prescribed for a third grade certificate. An average grade of seventy-five (75) per cent. shall be required, with a grade in no branch below fifty (50) per cent.

Amendment Second Grade.

SEC. 3. That Section 7, of Chapter 4192, of the Laws of Florida be, and the same is hereby amended to read as follows: An applicant for a first grade certificate shall be examined in civil government, algebra and physical geography, in addition to the branches required for a third grade certificate. An applicant for a first grade certificate must make an average grade of eighty (80) per cent. and shall grade in no branch below sixty (60) per cent.

Amendment First Grade.

SEC. 4. That Section 8, of Chapter 4192, of the Laws of Florida be, and the same is hereby amended to read as follows: A State certificate shall be issued only by the State Superintendent of Public Instruction to persons holding a first grade certificate and who have taught at least twenty-four (24) months, (eight months of which must have been taught in this State successfully under a first grade certificate). The

State Certificate.

Superintendent of Public Instruction shall issue no State certificate except on written examination in the following branches: Geometry, trigonometry, physics, zoology, botany, Latin, rhetoric, English literature, mental science, and general history. A candidate for a State certificate must make an average grade on the prescribed branches of eighty-five (85) per cent., with the grade in no branch below sixty (60) per cent.

SEC. 5. That Section 9, of Chapter 4192, of the Laws of Florida, be and the same is hereby amended to read as follows: Any teacher holding a State certificate issued under this Act, and such of Chapter 4192 of the Laws of Florida as are not hereby repealed, and who has taught successfully in a high school in this State for the period of thirty (30) months, may be granted a life certificate by the State Superintendent without further examination, if endorsed by three persons holding State certificates as possessing eminent teaching ability, and as having been eminently successful in governing and conducting a school.

Life Certificate.

SEC. 6. That Section 12, of Chapter 4192, of the Laws of Florida, be and the same is hereby amended to read as follows: The County Board of Public Instruction, prior to any authorized examination, shall appoint three teachers holding the highest grade certificate among the teachers of the county as a grading committee; said committee shall, immediately after the close of any examination, carefully examine and grade each paper turned over to it by the County Superintendent. When the said committee shall have completed its work it shall deliver back to the County Superintendent all papers turned over to it, with a gradation sheet showing the grade of each examinee in each branch upon which he or she was examined, also the average grade and rank of each examinee. The County Superintendent shall then, for the first time, make known to the grading committee the names corresponding to the number of any examinee, and shall then, in the presence of said committee, present his list and write on said gradation sheet the name of each examinee after his or her proper number. The said grading committee shall retain one copy of said gradation sheet, and shall file one with the County Superintendent, who shall issue certificates to the examinees, making averages according to the provisions of Sections 1, 2 and 3 of this Act, and to no others.

Grading Committee.

SEC. 7. That section 16, of Chapter 4192, of the Laws of Florida, be and the same is hereby amended to read as follows: Third grade certificates shall be good only in the county in which they are issued.

Third Grade Certificates, where good.

Second Grade Certificates, where good.

SEC. 8. That Section 17, of Chapter 4192, of the laws of Florida, be and the same is hereby amended to read as follows: First and second grade certificates may be indorsed by the County Superintendent of any county in the State, and shall then be good in the county in which it is endorsed as well as the one in which it was issued.

Examinations.

SEC. 9. That Section 19, of Chapter 4192, of the Laws of Florida, be and the same is hereby amended to read as follows: There shall be held two examinations a year in each county in the State, beginning on Tuesday after the first Monday in June and September, and each may continue one or more days at the discretion of the examiner and a vote of the examinees; *Provided*, That only one examination may be held

Proviso.

in any county if two be found unnecessary; *Provided, further*, That County Superintendents may hold a special examination, and issue temporary certificates for a term of not longer than the interval between the regular examinations, provided the applicant for such certificate furnishes satisfactory reasons for having failed to attend the regular examination.

SEC. 10. A third grade certificate shall be good for two years from date of issue. A second grade certificate shall be

Time Certificates are good.

good for three years from date of issue, and a first grade certificate shall be good for four years from date of issue. And all certificates granted in accordance with the provisions of this Act, and such of Chapter 4192 of the Laws of Florida as are not hereby repealed, shall be re-issuable upon examination.

SEC. 11. That at least one of the examinations of teachers shall be held at the county seat of the county in which the examination is held; *Provided*, That where two examinations are

One examination at county seat.

held the County Board of Public Instruction may designate another convenient place for holding one of such examinations other than the county site.

Who entitled to benefits.

SEC. 12. That all persons holding certificates granted in accordance with the provisions of Chapter 4192 of the Laws of Florida, shall be entitled to all the benefits and governed by the provisions of this Act.

SEC. 13. That any person holding a diploma of graduation from either of the State Normal Colleges of this State, upon

Diplomas of Graduation.

presentation of said diploma to any County Superintendent in this State, shall be entitled to a first grade certificate without examination; *Provided*, The person holding such diploma applies for such certificates within one year from the granting of such diploma.

SEC. 14. All laws and parts of laws in conflict with this Act
are hereby repealed.

SEC. 15. This act shall take effect upon its passage and approval by the Governor.

Approved June 3, 1895.

CHAPTER 4332.—[No. 11.]

AN ACT Requiring the Boards of Public Instruction for the Several
Counties of this State and Treasurers of County School Funds, to
make and Publish Itemized Financial Statements of their Dealings
with County School Funds.

Be it Enacted by the Legislature of the State of Florida:

SECTION 1. It shall be the duty of the treasurer of the
school fund of each county in this State by the first Monday
in each and every month, to prepare and file with the County
Superintendent of Public Instruction of his county, a detailed
and itemized statement in writing, showing all sums of money
received by such treasurer during the month next preceding,
and from whom and from what source received, and all
amounts by him paid out during such time and to whom paid,
and describing by date, number and amount of all warrants
paid.

Duty of Treas-
urer of Schoo
Fund.

SEC. 2. It shall be the duty of the Boards of Public Instruction of the several counties of this State to prepare and file
with the Clerks of the Circuit Court of their counties, respectively, by the first Monday in August, A. D. 1895, a detailed
and itemized financial statement in writing showing all sums
of money received on account of county school funds for and
during the year next preceding, and from whom received, and
from what source derived. And all amounts paid out during
such year, to whom and on what account paid. What funds,
if any, are on hand, and what indebtedness, if any is outstanding. Such statement shall be certified by the treasurer
of the county school fund and attested by the County Superintendent of Public Instruction, and in all counties where a
newspaper exists, the Board of Public Instruction shall cause
said statement to be published; *Provided*, The cost of such
publication shall not exceed ten dollars to be paid out of the
county school fund. Otherwise they shall have the same
posted at the court house and at three other public places in
the county.

Duty of
Boards of
Public In-
struction.

SEC. 3. It shall be the duty of each and every Board of
Public Instruction of the several counties of this State to prepare and file with the Clerk of the Circuit Court of their re-

To file itemized
financial state-
ment.

spective counties by the first Tuesday after the first Monday in September, A. D. 1895, and by the corresponding Tuesday in each and every month thereafter, an itemized financial statement showing all sums of money received during the month next preceding, on account of county school funds, and from whom received, and from what source derived. All appropriations made by such board and for what purpose made. All warrants drawn by such board, in whose favor and for and on what account drawn, describing such warrant by date, number and amount. All such monthly financial statements shall be certified by the Chairman of the Board of Public Instruction for the county and attested by the County Superintendent of Public Instruction, and the said board shall without delay cause the same to be published in a newspaper of the county, when any such newspaper exists; *Provided*, The cost

Proviso.

of such monthly publication shall not exceed two dollars per month, otherwise they shall post the same at the court house and at three other public places in the county.

SEC. 4. The financial statements of account hereinbefore provided for, when filed with the Clerk of the Circuit Court,

To be filed with Clerk.

shall be securely kept by him and shall at all times be open to the examination and inspection of the people of the county without fee or charge.

SEC. 5. Members of Boards of Public Instruction, County Superintendents of Public Instruction, and treasurers of county school funds who shall fail or refuse to perform any of the

Penalty.

duties required of them by the provisions of this act, shall for such neglect of duty be subject and liable to suspension and removal from office by the Governor under the provisions of Section 15, of Article 4, of the Constitution.

SEC. 6. This action shall take effect from the date of its approval by the Governor.

Approved May 30, 1895.

CHAPTER 4333—[No. 12.]

AN ACT to Authorize and Require the County Board of Public Instruction of Monroe County to have the English Language Taught in San Carlos Public School.

Be it Enacted by the Legislature of the State of Florida:

SECTION 1. The County Board of Public Instruction of Monroe county are hereby authorized and required to employ a competent teacher to instruct the Cuban pupils of the San

Carlos School, in the City of Key West, in the elements of the English language.

Sec. 2. The said Board of Public Instruction shall make provision for the payment of the salary of teachers so employed, out of the common school fund of said Monroe county.

Sec. 3. This act shall take effect from and after its passage and approval by the Governor.

Approved May 31, 1895.

Chapter 4334—[No. 13.]

AN ACT to Establish at Bartow, Florida. The South Florida Military and Educational Institute, and to Provide an Appropriation therefor.

Be it Enacted by the Legislature of the State of Florida:

Section 1. The South Florida Military and Educational Institute is hereby established at Bartow, Polk county, Florida, under the direction and control of the State Board of Education, who shall elect such faculty as may be required to carry out the provisions of this act.

Sec. 2. The design of this institution is to teach such branches of learning, including military tactics, as may be required by the State Board of Education.

Design

Sec. 3. Each Senator, during his term of office, shall be empowered to nominate, upon competitive examination, one student, who shall be a resident of his Senatorial District, to said South Florida Military and Educational Institute, who shall be entitled to receive the benefit of a full course of instruction at said Institute without any charge for board, lodging, tuition, use of text-books, washing, fuel, lights and use of arms and equipments. Said students to be subject to such rules and regulations as may be established for the government and direction of said Institute.

Senators to nominate students.

Sec. 4. That for the purpose of carrying out the provisions of this act the sum of sixty-four hundred dollars ($6,400.00) be, and the same is hereby apportioned for each two ensuing years, commencing September 1, 1895, out of any moneys in the State Treasury not otherwise appropriated.

Appropriation.

Sec. 5. That this act shall take effect upon its approval by the Governor.

Approved May 29, 1895.

CHAPTER 4335—[No. 14.]

AN ACT to Prohibit White and Negro Youth from being Taught in the Same Schools.

Be it Enacted by the Legislature of the State of Florida:

SECTION 1. It shall be a penal offense for any individual, body of individuals, corporation or association to conduct within this State any school of any grade, public, private or parochial wherein white persons and negroes shall be instructed or boarded within the same building, or taught in the same class, or at the same time by the same teacher.

SEC. 2. Any person or persons violating the provisions of Section 1 of this Act, by patronizing or teaching in such school shall upon conviction thereof be fined in a sum not less than $150.00 nor more than $500.00, or imprisoned in the county jail for not less than three months nor more than six months for every such offense.

Penalty.

SEC. 3. All laws or parts of laws in conflict with the provisions of this act are hereby repealed.

SEC. 4. This act shall take effect September 1st, 1895.

Approved May 29, 1895.

CHAPTER 4336—[No. 15.]

AN ACT to Provide for the Division of Counties into Convenient School Sub-Districts, and for the Election Bi-ennially of Three School Trustees, and for the Levying and Collection of a District School Tax, and Providing for the Holding of Elections for such Purposes.

Be it Enacted by the Legislature of the State of Florida:

SECTION 1. That an election may be held in any city, town, community, section or division of any county, under the order and direction of the Board of Public Instruction of any county upon the petition of one-fourth of the registered and qualified voters of any such city, town, community, section or division of such county, who are tax-payers on real or personal property therein, to determine whether such city, town, community, section or division of such county, shall be a school sub-district, and for the election of three trustees therefor, and to determine the millage to be assessed and collected annually during the succeeding two years. Such election shall be held and the result ascertained and declared as nearly as practicable in the same manner as is provided by law for the holding of elections concerning Article

XIX of the Constitution, substituting the Board of Public Instruction for the County Commissioners. It shall require a majority of the votes of those voting at any such election to determine any matter in the affirmative. At an election to decide whether such sub-district shall be formed three school trustees shall be elected to serve as such, should a majority of the electors vote for and create such sub-district, and on the same day bi-ennially thereafter, and at each of such elections the millage to be assessed and collected annually during the succeeding two years for school purposes in such sub-district shall be determined by a majority vote of the qualified electors as herein provided. Notice of holding any such election to determine whether such city, town, community, section or other division of such county, shall be made a school sub-district, or for the election of school trustees, shall be made by the Board of Public Instruction by publishing a notice in a newspaper published in such city, town, community, section or other division of such county to be made a school sub-district, for four consecutive weeks; *Provided*, That the cost of such publication shall be paid by the school sub-districts respectively, or by posting such notice in three public places, within the limits of such city, town, community, section or other division to be made a sub-district, for thirty days prior thereto.

SEC. 2. All voters in such election for sub-districts or trustees shall have the qualifications specified in section one for petitioners for elections to establish sub-districts.

SEC. 3. The petition mentioned in section one of this Act shall fix and define the boundary of the city, town and adjacent territory, community, section or other division intended to be made and formed into a school sub-district, which boundary shall include but one public school, except in incorporated towns.

SEC. 4. It shall be the duty of the trustees on or before the last Monday in July of each year to prepare an itemized estimate, showing the amount of money required for necessary common school purpose of their sub-district for the next ensuing scholastic year; stating the rate of millage to be assessed and collected upon the taxable property of their sub-district to cover such amount, not to exceed three mills on the dollar. A copy of the intemized estimate herein provided for shall be filed with the Clerk of the Board of County Commissioners, which Board shall direct the Assessor of Taxes to assess, and the Collector to collect, the amount so stated. Moneys collected under the provisions of this Act shall be paid over to the trustees of the sub-district in which the tax is levied.

Sidenotes:
1899.
Majority of those voting required.
Proviso.
Qualification.
Boundary.
Duty of Trustees.
Disposition of money.

Object

A corporation.

Trustees to give bond.

SEC. 5. The object of a school sub-district shall be to promote the school interest of the district, when formed, by the collection and judicious appropriation of a special school tax.

SEC. 6. They shall also be a corporation with the usual powers for the purpose of performing their duties.

SEC. 7. They shall receive and hold the money which may be assessed and collected as hereinbefore provided as a special tax, to be disbursed in the district where collected, solely for school purposes. These trustees shall be required to give bond in twice the amount raised by the special tax, to be approved by the Board of Public Instruction before receiving any such money.

SEC. 8. All laws and parts of laws in conflict herewith are hereby repealed.

SEC. 9. This act shall take effect upon its approval by the Governor.

Approved May 20, 1895.

CHAPTER 4337—[No 16.]

AN ACT to Amend Section 3 Chapter 4194, Laws of Florida, Entitled an Act to Provide for School Sub-Districts in Counties and Towns, and to Provide for the Levying and Collection of Taxes for the Support of Schools in such Sub-Districts, Approved June 2, 1893.

Be it Enacted by the Legislature of the State of Florida:

SECTION 1. That Section 3 of Chapter 4194 be amended so as to read as follows:

Duty of Trustees.

SEC. 3. It shall be the duty of these trustees on or before the last Monday in June of each year to prepare an itemized estimate, showing the amount of money required for the necessary common school purposes of their sub-district for the next ensuing scholastic year; stating the rate of millage to be assessed and collected upon the taxable property of their sub-district to cover such amount, not to exceed three mills on the dollar. A copy of the itemized estimate herein provided for shall be filed with the Clerk of the Board of County Commissioners and the Comptroller of the State, and it shall become the duty of the Comptroller to assess all railroads and railroad property situated in such school sub-district upon the filing with him by the County Commissioners a copy of the amount to be assessed by the County Commissioners, and the Comptroller shall collect the amount so assessed by the County Commissioners in such sub-district and pay over the same to the trustees of such sub-district.

Sec. 2. All laws in conflict with this amendment are hereby repealed.

Approved June 1, 1895.

CHAPTER 4362—[No. 41.]

AN ACT to Amend Sctions 272, 273, 274 of the Revised Statutes of Florida, Relative to the Powers and Duties of the Board of Managers of State Blind, Deaf and Mute Institute.

Be it Enacted by the Legislature of the State of Florida:

SECTION 1. That Section 272 of the Revised Statutes of Florida be amended to read as follows:

Section 272. Said Board of Managers shall provide for the education, care and maintenance at said asylum of all persons residing in this State between the ages of six and twenty-one years, who may be blind, or deaf and dumb. *[Duty Board of Managers.]*

SEC. 2. That Section 273 of the Revised Statutes of the State of Florida be amended to read as follows:

Section 273. Any person entitled to admission into said Institute, or the parent, guardian or next friend of such person, may apply to the Board of County Commissioners of the county of his residence, and the County Commissioners, if satisfied that the person is so entitled to such admission, shall issue a certificate to that effect, upon which the applicant shall be received into the asylum. *[County Commissioners issue certificate to admit.]*

SEC. 3. That Section 274 of the Revised Statutes of the State of Florida be amended to read as follows:

Section 274. Said Board of County Commissioners shall supply means of transportation of such persons to said asylum, and at the close of each session the Board of Managers shall supply means of transportation for the inmates to their respective homes and return at the opening of the next succeeding session. The same to be paid for out of the general appropriation for the maintenance of said asylum; those who have the means will be required to pay the necessary expenses, tuition excepted, of their children or wards. *[Transportation.]*

SEC. 4. All laws or parts of laws in conflict herewith are hereby repealed.

Sec. 5. This act shall take effect upon its passage and approval by the Governor.

Approved May 31, 1895.

ELECTION OF COUNTY BOARDS OF PUBLIC INSTRUCTION.

Extract from the General Election Law, being Chapter 4328, Laws of Florida, approved June 1st, 1895.

Section 3. * * * A County Board of Public Instruction consisting of three members, one member from each School Board District elected from the several counties at large of this State, shall be chosen at the general election A. D. 1896, and at every general election thereafter, unless changed by law.

CHAPTER 4566—[No. 52.]

AN ACT to Provide for Teachers' Summer Schools, and to Make Appropriations Therefor.

Whereas, The value of the public schools must be measured by the character of the teachers employed; and

Whereas, Teachers' Summer Schools have been recognized in all the States as one of the most potent means of improving the work of those engaged in teaching, by awakening greater interest and enthusiasm in their work and in improving their scholarship and suggesting the best methods of instruction; and *Preamble.*

Whereas, The Trustees of the Peabody Fund have deemed money expended in the direction of improving the teaching force as the wisest disposition of their trust in distributing its benefits to all the children, and have demanded that the Legislature make an appropriation to supplement their donation for this particular branch of school work; therefore

Be it Enacted by the Legislature of the State of Florida:

SECTION 1. That the sum of three thousand dollars for the year of 1897, and three thousand dollars for the year 1898, be, and the same is hereby, appropriated for the purpose of *Appropriation.* holding as many Teachers' Summer Schools at such times and places as the State Superintendent of Public Instruction may designate, and as the fund appropriated and donated by the Peabody Trustees will sustain.

SEC. 2. That impartial provision shall be made for the instruction of teachers of both races in these Summer Schools for the period of two months, and the sums appropriated in *Appropriation subject to order of State Superintendent of Public Instruction.* the foregoing section shall be subject to the order of the State Superintendent of Public Instruction, and paid upon requisition of said Superintendent upon the Comptroller, out of any money in the State Treasury, not otherwise appropriated.

SEC. 3. It shall be the duty of the State Superintendent of Public Instruction to submit a report to the next General *Duty of State Superintendent of Public Instruction.* Assembly, showing where and the number of such Summer Schools conducted, the number of teachers attending each by

5

sex and race, the number of conductors of each school, the
number of days service rendered by each, and submit vouchers for every dollar of the fund paid out.

SEC. 4. Any laws in conflict with this act is repealed by this
act.

CHAPTER 4567—[No. 53.]

AN ACT to Amend Section 5, of Chapter 4193, Laws of Florida,
Being an Act Fixing the Salaries and Mileage of the County
School Boards.

Be it Enacted by the Legislature of the State of Florida:

SECTION 1. That Section 5 of Chapter 4193, Laws of Florida, be amended to read as follows:

The members of the various County School Boards shall be
Salary and mileage of members of County School Boards. paid from the county school fund for their services, two dollars per day, for each days service, and ten cents per mile for
every mile actually traveled in going to and from the county
court house by the nearest practical route.

SEC. 2. That all laws or parts of laws in conflict with this
act be and the same are hereby repealed.

Approved June 4, 1897.

CHAPTER 4568—[No. 54.]

AN ACT to Amend Sections 3 and 4, Chapter 4334, Laws of Florida,
Entitled an Act to Establish at Bartow, Florida, The South Florida
Military and Educational Institute and to Provide and Appropri-
ate Therefor, Approved May 29, 1895.

Be it Enacted by the Legislature of the State of Florida:

SECTION 1. That Section 3 of Chapter forty-three hundred
and thirty-four be amended so as to read as follows:

SECTION 3. The Representatives from each county in connection with the Senator representing said county shall be
Manner of selecting student for free tuition, etc. empowered to name upon competitive examination and in
such manner as the State Board of Education may prescribe,
one student for each county who shall be resident in said
county to the said South Florida Military and Educational
Institute who shall be entitled to receive the benefit of a full
course of instruction at said Institute without charge for

board, lodging, tuition, use of text books, washing, fuel, lights and use of arms and equipments. Said student to be subject to such rules and regulations as may be established for the government and direction of said institution.

SEC. 2. That Section 4 of Chapter forty-three hundred and thirty-four be amended so as to read as follows:

SEC. 4. That for the purpose of carrying out the provisions of this act the sum of nine thousand dollars ($9,000) be and the same is hereby appropriated for each of the two ensuing years commencing September 1, 1897, out of any moneys in the State Treasury not otherwise appropriated.

SEC. 3. All laws and parts of law in conflict with these amendments are hereby repealed.

Approved June 1, 1897.

SESSION LAWS OF 1899.

CHAPTER 4678—[No. 17.]

AN ACT to Provide for the Division of Counties into School Districts, and for the Election Bi-ennially of three School Trustees, and to Prescribe their Duties and Powers, and for Levying, Collecting and Disbursing District School Taxes.

Be it Enacted by the Legislature of the State of Florida:

School unit.

School District.

Special tax Schools.

SECTION 1. That each county shall constitute a school unit; that all sub-divisions of a county for school purposes shall be designated as school districts; all school districts levying a school district tax shall hereafter be designated as special tax school districts, and all schools receiving any district tax, as special tax schools.

Board of Public Instruction to order election.

Special Tax School District.

Matters to be determined by election.

Trustees special tax school district.

Proviso.

SEC. 2. It shall be the duty of the Board of Public Instruction of any county to order an election to be held in any sub-division of any city or incorporated town, community or sub-division of the county, at such time and place as said Board may direct, whenever one-fourth of the qualified electors that pay a tax on real or personal property, and are resident in such city, incorporated town, community, or sub-division of the county, shall petition for such election, to determine whether such city, incorporated town, community or sub-division of the county shall become a special tax school district for the purpose of levying and collecting a district school tax for the exclusive use of public free schools within the district; at such election the following matters shall be determined by a majority of the ballots cast by electors qualified as herein prescribed, except that the three persons receiving the highest vote at such election shall be declared School Trustees of said district: First, whether the city, incorporated town, community or sub-division of the county shall become a special tax school district; Second, who shall be the School Trustees of said district; Third, the number of mills of district tax to be levied and collected annually for the two succeeding years. The three persons receiving the highest number of votes cast shall be declared the Trustees elected for the special tax school district; provided, a majority of all the votes cast be in favor of creating such special tax district, who shall serve for the next ensuing two years and perform the duties hereinafter prescribed.

SEC. 3. The petition mentioned above in this act shall prescribe the boundaries of the sub-division of any city, or city, incorporated town, community or sub-division of the county intended to be formed into a special tax school district. The Board of Public Instruction may, however, change the boundaries thereof before ordering any such election; but shall in no case include territory not included in original petition, and shall give notice of any such change in the notice of election. Special tax school districts created under this act, shall continue until dis-established or changed by like proceeding as those by which they were created. The petition provided for by Section 2 of this act shall be published once a week, for four (4) successive weeks, in some newspaper published in the county having a general circulation throughout the county; and the publication shall state when such petition shall be presented to such Boards. In case there shall be no newspaper published in the county, such petition and notice shall be posted in the manner provided in Section 4 of this act for the posting of notice of election.

What petition must prescribe.

Publication of petition.

SEC. 4. It shall be the duty of the Board of Public Instruction of the county to cause a notice of said election to be published once a week for four successive weeks prior thereto in a newspaper published within the county, and having a general circulation throughout the county; but if no newspaper be published in said county, then it shall cause five written or printed notices of said election to be posted in five public places within the territory in which the election is ordered. It shall also be the duty of the County Board of Public Instruction to appoint inspectors and clerks for said election, whose duties shall be the same as those of similar officers in general elections, except as herein stated.

Notice of election to be published.

Inspectors and clerks.

SEC. 5. The Board of Public Instruction shall canvass the returns of election as made to it by the inspectors and clerks of election, and declare the results at the next regular meeting of said Board, or at a special meeting called for that purpose.

Canvass of returns.

SEC. 6. All special tax school district elections shall be held and conducted in the manner prescribed by law for holding general elections, except as provided in this act, and it is hereby made the duty of the Supervisor of Registration of any county to furnish, upon payment for such service, to the County Board of Public Instruction, on demand, a certified list of the qualified voters residing in a special tax school district, or the territory to be created into a special tax school

Manner of holding election.

1899.

district, that have paid a tax on real or personal property for the year next preceding any such special tax election.

Who entitled to vote.

SEC. 7. All qualified voters residing within the territory sought to be made a special tax school district that pay a tax on real or personal property shall be entitled to vote in said election, and a majority of the votes cast shall determine any matter voted upon, pertaining to a special tax school district.

County Board of Public Instruction to pay expenses of election.

The cost of the publication of the notice of such election, and of the election itself, shall be paid by the County Board of Public Instruction out of the first moneys collected from the special tax district.

Elec'l'n to be held bi ennially.

SEC. 8. Elections shall be held bi-ennially in each special tax school district, as near as practicable upon the anniversary of the original election, under the direction of the County Board of Public Instruction, to determine who shall be Trustees for the succeeding two years, and the number of mills of district school tax to be levied for each of said years; said elections shall be held under the same rules and regulations, and qualifications of electors shall be the same as prescribed for those voting in the original election creating a special tax school district.

Trustees have supervision of public schools.

Trustees to perform duties of Supervisor.

Removal of Trustees.

SEC. 9. Whenever a special tax school district is created and Trustees are elected, they shall have the supervision of all the public schools within said district. The position of Supervisor shall be superseded by that of Trustees, and the duties prescribed by law for Supervisors shall be performed by the Trustees. The powers of Trustees shall not be those of control, but of supervision only, and shall extend to all the public schools within the special district. Any Trustee failing to discharge the duties of the position shall be removed, after due notice to such Trustee, by the County Board of Public Instruction, and all vacancies occurring in the Board of Trustees from any cause, shall be filled for the unexpired term by the County Board of Public Instruction, upon nomination by the patrons of the school.

Schools to be under control of County Board of Public Instruction and County Superintendent.

Proviso.

SEC. 10. All public schools conducted within a special tax school district shall be under the direction and control of the County Board of Public Instruction and County Superintendent as in other districts, and subject to the same laws, rules and regulations prescribed for the conduct of other schools, except that the Trustees shall have the power to nominate to the County Board of Public Instruction teachers for all schools within such special district; *Provided*, That no person be nominated for teacher who does not ho ld a teach er's certificate unimpaired by suspension, revocation or limitation, or that will not remain in full force for the term of school, and obtained in compliance with the laws of the State. The County Board of Public Instruction shall have the right to reject any teacher nominated, and in case the second nomination of a teacher for any position be not ratified, the said Board shall then proceed on its own motion, to fill vacancies in the teaching force in any school in the special tax school district.

County Board Public Instruction right to reject any teacher.

SEC. 11. The Board of Trustees shall have the further right to say what proportion of the school funds raised within the district shall be applied in any year to building, repairs on buildings, to school libraries, to salaries of teachers, and to other educational purposes; *Provided*, That they shall make a fair and equitable distribution of the funds among all the schools in the special tax school district, which shall be shown in their itemized estimate.

Powers of Trustees.

SEC. 12. It shall be the duty of these Trustees, on or before the first day of June in each year, to prepare an itemized estimate, showing the amount of money necessary and likely to be raised for the supplement of the county school funds appropriated to the district for the next ensuing scholastic year, and to certify therein the rate of millage voted to be assessed and collected upon the taxable property within the special tax school district for that year. This estimate shall set forth clearly the apportionment of money raised within the district pro rated to each school within the district, stating the amount that will be applied to the salaries of teachers, buildings, furniture or for other educational purposes. It shall also state the number of miles of railroad track and telegraph lines within the bounds of the district. This itemized estimate shall be made in triplicate, one copy to be filed with the Clerk of the Board of County Commissioners, one copy with the Comptroller of the State, one copy with the County Board of Public Instruction; *Provided*, That where there are no railroad or telegraph lines in such district such itemized estimate need not be furnished to the Comptroller. It shall be the duty of the County Commissioners to order the Assessor to assess, and the Collector to collect the amount legally assessed upon the property of the special district, at the rate of millage designated by the Board of Trustees, and pay the same to the County Treasurer; it shall be the duty of the Comptroller of the State to assess all railroads and railroad property, together with telegraph lines and telegraph property situated in

Duty of Trustees.

Duty of County Commissioners.

Duty of Comptroller.

Duty of
County Board
of Public In-
struction.

County Treas-
urer liable for
special tax.

Special tax
fund.

Proviso

Trustees to be
a corporation

Proviso.

such school special district, and to collect the taxes thereon in the same manner as required by law to assess and collect said taxes for State and county purposes, and to remit the same to the Treasurer of the counties, to be by them held to the credit of each special tax school district fund and to be paid out as hereinafter provided. It shall be the duty of the County Board of Public Instruction to add the amount set apart for the salaries of teachers in each school within the special tax school district to the county appropriation made for that school, and upon this determine the salaries to be paid teachers and the length of the term that the school shall continue, and contract with teachers for the full term that said fund, arising from both county appropriation and the special tax fund, will sustain the school. The part of this fund arising from the special tax shall be paid to the teachers upon the order of the County Board based upon reports approved by the Trustees, the same as other school funds are paid upon the endorsement of school Supervisors. The County Treasurer shall be liable for all special tax school district funds upon his official bond, after receiving said funds, as in the case of other county revenues.

SEC. 13. The special tax fund set apart by the Board of Trustees for the payment of teachers shall not be subject to requisition for any other purpose by said Trustees; the funds estimated for other educational purposes shall be paid out by warrants of the Board of Public Instruction of the county upon the County Treasurer, said warrants to be based upon requisitions made by the Board of Trustees accompanied by itemized bills for things purchased or work performed. All special funds collected within a school district shall be disbursed solely for school purposes within the district in which collected, and, as near as practicable, in the year in which the tax is collected, upon the recommendation of the Board of Trustees; *Provided,* That the Trustees shall make no contract with one of its members embracing any monetary consideration.

SEC. 14. The Trustees of any school district shall be a corporation and may hold property, sue and be sued, and perform other corporate functions, and perform the usual duties necessary to provide buildings, repair the same, and to purchase libraries and other school appliances; *Provided,* That no debt shall be created without the approval of the County Board of Public Instruction.

Sec. 15. Nothing in this act shall have the effect to abrogate or anywise impair any existing school sub-district, but
he same are hereafter to be governed by this act.

Not to effect
existing school
sub-districts.

Sec. 16. Children residing outside of any special tax school
district shall not attend school in any such district without
he consent of the Trustees thereof, and of the County Board
of Public Instruction; *Provided,* That nothing in this act
shall be so construed as to prevent attendance from an adjoining county, provided the County School Board of such
adjoining county shall pay a pro rata share of such attendance. Such pro rata share to be estimated by the Trustees of
uch school where such attendance is made; *Provided further,*
That pupils from other districts or sub-districts shall be sub-
ect to same conditions as pupils from other counties as pro-
ided in this act.

Children out-
side of special
tax
school district.

Proviso.

Proviso.

Sec. 17. Each voter voting at any election under this act
hall vote but one ballot, and the same shall be written, or
printed in black ink on plain white paper, and be substantially
of the following form, according as he may desire to vote
upon any, or all of the questions submitted:

As to voting.

'or (or Against) Special Tax School District..............,....
'chool Trustees (Stating their names)....................
....
....
... .
Maximum Tax Levy: .... mills.

Sec. 18. All laws or parts of laws inconsistent with this act
.re hereby repealed.

Sec. 19. This act shall take effect thirty days after its pas-
age and approval by the Governor.

Approved June 5, 1899.

CHAPTER 4679—[No. 18.]

AN ACT to Amend Section 260, of the Revised Statutes of the
State of Florida, entitled "Census by Supervisors" and Section
261. of such Revised Statutes, entitled "On Failure of Supervisors,
Superintendent to Take Census."

Be it Enacted by the Legislature of the State of Florida:

Section 1. That Section 260 of the such Revised Statutes,
uch section being entitled, Census by Supervisor, be and the
ame is hereby amended so as to read as follows:

1899.

County Super-
intendent to
take census.

260. Census by Superintendent.—It shall be the duty of the County Superintendent of Public Instruction of each county before the 15th day of May in the year 1900, and every ten years thereafter, to take the census of all children in his county, between the ages of 6 and 21 years; and if any such children be idiots, or insane, or blind, or deaf mutes he shall so state, and he shall report such census to the School Board of the county, and to the State Superintendent of Public Instruction, on or before the first day of June of the year in which such census shall be taken. He shall certify to such report as being correct,

Penalty for
failure to per-
form duty.

and shall be paid three cents for each child so reported, and upon his failing to perform the duties herein required of him, he shall be relieved from office. In case he shall employ any person or persons to assist in making any such enumeration of such children, such person or persons shall make a sworn statement showing when and where such enumeration was made, and that the same is correct, and the same shall be filed by the Superintendent with the School Board as part of his report.

SEC. 6. That said Section 261 of said Revised Statutes is hereby amended so as to read as follows:

261. On the Failure of Superintendent, the County School

County School
Board to have
duties per-
formed on
failure of
County Super-
intendent.

Board to Have Census Taken.—In case the County Superintendent of Schools shall fail to perform any duty imposed upon him by the preceding section, as and when the same is required to be performed, it shall be the duty of the County School Board to cause the same to be done as soon as practicable by some person or persons to be selected by such Board.

Approved June 5, 1899.

CHAPTER 4680—[No. 19.]

AN ACT to Provide for County Adoptions of Uniformity of Text Books in the Public Free Schools of this State.

Be it Enacted by the Legislature of the State of Florida :

SECTION 1. It shall be the duty of the County Boards of

Uniform sys-
tem of school
books.

Public Instruction to put in operation in the public free schools in their respective counties a uniform system of school books; but however, that the adoption of such system shall be gradual and not sooner made than the interests of the pupils and patrons may dictate; *And Provided,* That the entire adoption shall be consummated by July 1, 1901.

SEC. 2. The selection of books to constitute such uniform system in each county shall be made by the County Board of Public Instruction of the county, who before deciding upon any book or books shall consult with the County Superintendent of Public Schools and at least three leading teachers of the county. Before any adoption shall be made at least sixty days' previous notice of the time and place such adoption will considered published once a week for three successive weeks in some newspaper having a general circulation throughout the county, or in the absence of such newspaper to be posted in at least five different and conspicuous places in the county shall be given by the School Board; any adoption made hereunder shall last at least five years. The County Superintendent shall see that the books adopted are used by the pupils and the teachers shall not use any other books in teaching.

Selection of books to be made by County Boards.

Notice of adoption to be given by School Board.

SEC. 3. Nothing in this act shall have the effect to interfere with or impair any entire or partial adoption heretofore made and now existing in any county of the State.

Where act does not interfere.

SEC. 4. This act shall take effect immediately upon its approval by the Governor.

Approved June 5, 1899.

CHAPTER 4681—[No. 20.]

AN ACT to Provide for Teachers' Summer Schools, and to Make Appropriations Therefor.

Whereas, Dr. J. L. M. Curry, Agent of the Peabody Fund, has written the State Superintendent of Public Instruction that he "will gladly renew the appropriation for Teachers' Summer Schools to the extent of $1200, provided the Legislature will supplement it by an equal or greater sum," and there is and always will be a large proportion of the teachers in the public schools without professional training and poorly fitted for the work; therefore,

Preamble.

Be it Enacted by the Legislature of the State of Florida:

SECTION 1. That the sum of one thousand eight hunndred dollars for the year 1899, and one thousand eight hundred dollars for the year 1900, be, and the same is hereby

Appropriation for 1899 and 1900.

appropriated for the purpose of conducting as many Summer Schools for teachers, at such times and places as the State Superintendent of Public Instruction may deem best, and as the fund appropriated and donated by the Peabody Trustees will sustain. And the sums appropriated shall be paid by the Treasurer on the warrant of Comptroller to the teachers of said Summer Schools upon vouchers approved by the State Superintendent accompanied with a certificate of the County Superintendent of the county in which such school has been taught, that the service charged for has been rendered, such accounts to be audited by the Comptroller before payment.

SEC. 2. That impartial provision shall be made for the instruction of teachers of both races in these Summer Schools, and the sums appropriated in the foregoing section shall be subject to the order of the State Superintendent of Public Instruction, and paid upon requisition of said Superintendent upon the Comptroller out of any money in the State Treasury not otherwise appropriated.

Instruction of teachers of both races.

SEC. 3. It shall be the duty of the State Superintendent of Public Instruction to submit a report to the next General Assembly showing the number and location of such schools, the number of teachers attending each, by sex and race, the number of instructors employed in each school, the number of days' service rendered by each, and submit vouchers for for every dollar of the fund paid out.

Duty of State Superintendent.

SEC. 4. Any laws in conflict with this act are hereby repealed.

Approved June 2, 1899.

CHAPTER 4682—[No. 21.]

AN ACT to Authorize the Board of Public Instruction of any County of the State of Florida to Contract Debts for the Purchase of Real Estate to be used for Educational Purposes, for the Erection of School Buildings, and to Provide for the Payment Thereof,

Be it Enacted by the Legislature of the State of Florida:

SECTION 1. That the Board of County Commissioners upon the request of the Board of Public Instruction after an affirmative vote of the qualified voters who are tax-payers therein and have paid all taxes due by them for two years next and preceding said election in any sub-school district or county which debt shall be a charge or lien only upon such sub-school district or county as the case may be, are hereby authorized to contract debts for the purchase of real estate to be used for educational purposes, for the erection of school buildings, and to pay such debts out of the current income of any year, or out of the income of succeeding years; *Provided*, That the necessary expense of maintaining the schools in any county during any year shall constitute the first claim against the school fund of that year.

SEC. 2. That the Board of County Commissioners upon the request of the Board of Public Instruction after an affirmative vote of the qualified voters who are tax-payers therein and have paid all taxes due by them for two years next and preceding said election in any sub-school district or county, which debt shall be a charge or lien only upon such sub-school district or county as the case may be, are hereby authorized to borrow money from time to time as occasion may require to discharge any debt or liability incurred for the purchase of real estate for educational purposes, for the erection of school buildings, and to pay the interest and principal out of the current income of any year, or out of the income of succeeding years; *Provided*, That the necessary expense of maintaining the schools in any county during any year shall constitute the first claim against the school fund of that year.

SEC. 3. This act shall go into effect immediately upon its passage and approval.

Approved June 1, 1899.

CHAPTER 4666—[No. 5.]

AN ACT Relating to the Collection of and Accounting for Poll Taxes Collected in this State.

Be it Enacted by the Legislature of the State of Florida:

SECTION 1. That from and after the passage of this act it shall be the duty of the Tax Collector in every county of this State to file on or before the tenth day of every month with the County School Board, a certified list of the names of all persons whose poll taxes were paid during the previous month, giving the year for which such payments were made. A copy of this list shall also be filed with the County Commissioners

1899.

Duty of School
Board.

with a receipt from the County Treasurer for the amount collected as such poll taxes. It shall be the duty of the School Board to examine at least twice each year the books and records of the Tax Collector which relate to the collection of poll taxes and said Board shall require prompt settlement for all poll taxes assessed, together with those not assessed but collected.

Penalty.

Any Tax Collector or member of a County School Board who shall neglect to comply with the provisions of this act shall be suspended from office.

Duty of
County Super-
intendent.

Duty of State
Superinten-
dent of Public
Instruction.

Sec. 2. It shall be the duty of the County Superintendent of Public Instruction, acting as Secretary of the County School Board, to make and forward monthly a certified copy of the monthly lists of persons who have paid their poll taxes, mentioned in Section 1 of this act, to the State Superintendent of Public Instruction, who shall file and preserve the same in his office as a part of the public records and furnish copies thereof when requested by citizens of this State.

Approved June 2, 1899.

REGULATIONS AND FORMS

State Board of Education.

1895.

DEPARTMENT OF PUBLIC INSTRUCTION,

TALLAHASSEE, FLA., Oct. 7, 1895.

In compliance with the provisions of Section 33, paragraphs 1st and 7th, the following Regulations, Instructions and Forms have been prescribed by the State Board of Education for the use and guidance of school officers and teachers. (*Vide* Section 3.)

REGULATIONS AND INSTRUCTIONS.

GENERAL.

REGULATION 1. Persons to be eligible to school offices or positions must be of good moral character, temperate, upright, responsible, competent, and in full sympathy with the public educational system of the State. *Eligibility to school office.*

REG. 2. All Rules and Regulations prescribed by County Boards of Public Instruction, not at variance with the Statutes or the Regulations and Instructions of the State Board of Education, shall have the full force and effect of law, and must be respected accordingly. *Force of Regulations.*

REG. 3. County school officers and teachers shall in all cases use the blanks, forms, registers, etc., prescribed and furnished by the State Department. *Use of blanks.*

COUNTY BOARDS OF PUBLIC INSTRUCTION.

REG. 4. Members of County Boards of Public Instruction before assuming the duties of the office, must be commissioned by the State Superintendent of Public Instruction. The Secretary of State, as soon as practicable after any general election, shall notify the State Superintendent of Public Instruction of the election of School Board members in each county, giving name, school Board District, and post-office address of each; and the State Superintendent, on or before the first day of January thereafter, shall issue and transmit commissions to said members elect.

REG. 5. County Boards of Public Instruction shall hold regular meetings, at least monthly, during the session of schools, when they shall examine carefully all teachers' reports, issue warrants, hear the report of the County Superintendent and transact other business.

REG. 6. County Boards of Public Instruction shall not issue a warrant to any teacher, until the monthly report of said teacher, on which the warrant is based, be made out in conformity with the blanks furnished, and in compliance with the directions given in the Teacher's Register.

REG. 7. County Boards of Public Instruction shall not contract with any person to teach a school who does not hold a Teacher's Certificate, unimpaired by suspension, revocation or limitation, and granted in accordance with law. Nor shall any person be entitled to compensation from the public fund until he has been employed and contracted with by a Board.

REG. 8. It is the duty of County Boards of Public Instruction to select, assign and contract with teachers. This duty can in no case be delegated to Supervisors or patrons; but the Supervisor may report to the County Board, for its consideration, the names of such teachers as he thinks best suited to the requirements of the school and most satisfactory to the patrons.

REG. 9. County Boards of Public Instruction shall, at the first regular meeting after the June examination in each year, proceed to assign teachers to schools for the ensuing scholastic year, selecting first from the list of teachers those holding State or County Certificates, salaries may be fixed and contracts entered into at a subsequent meeting. After the September examination, all vacancies that exist shall be filled in like manner.

Marginal notes:

To be commissioned by State Superintendent.

To hold regular meetings.

When to issue warrants.

When to contract with teachers.

To assign teachers.

When to assign teachers.

REG. 10. The State Board of Education earnestly admonishes County Boards of Public Instruction to exercise great caution in the employment of teachers, that they may not subject themselves to the charge of being influenced by personal or political favoritism, sectarianism, or by ties of relationship.

REG. 11. The State Board of Education calls the special attention of County Boards of Public Instruction to the duty of prescribing a uniform course of study for their schools, and grading the same, as provided in Sec. 40, Par. 14th, of the School Laws.

REG. 12. The State Board of Education recommends the adoption by County Boards of a system of Rules and Regulations for their guidance and for the government of schools, teachers, and pupils. Such Rules and Regulations, together with the prescribed course of study, should be printed in pamphlet form and copies of the same filed in the office of the State Department. The State Superintendent shall, upon request, furnish a copy of such pamphlet to other County Boards.

REG. 13. The State Board of Education recommends to County Boards of Public Instruction the adoption, for their several counties, of a regulation for the uniform observance of she Christmas holidays, suggesting that all schools suspend not later than December 24th, and resume not earlier than the following 2d day of January.

REG. 14. The State Board of Education names the first Friday of February of each year as ARBOR-DAY, which shall *not* be observed as a holiday, but shall be devoted to the planting of trees on school grounds or other appropriate public places, together with suitable exercises, lessons or lectures designed to interest and instruct the children in the care and cultivation of trees. No teacher should be allowed compensation for Arbor-Day, unless a prescribed number of trees has been properly planted and securely protected against injury.

REG. 15. County Boards of Public Instruction should adopt a regulation requiring pupils from other States, or from other counties, to pay a specified tuition fee to the teacher, to be by him paid to the County Superintendent, and reported by the latter to the County Board.

1899.

To avoid favoritism.

To prescribe uniform course of study.

To print rules and regulations, etc

Christmas holidays.

Arbor Day.

May require tuition fees.

6

1899.

To observe 3-mile limit.

Reg. 16. The attention of County Boards of Public Instruction is called to the fact that the law expressly prohibits the establishing of schools, for the same race, nearer than three miles of each other, unless made necessary by local geographical features. Where this law has been violated in the past, it is the duty of County Boards to proceed as speedily as consistent with the interest of all concerned, to combine two or more schools into one, when practicable, or otherwise re arrange them so as to conform to the provisions of Sec. 40, Par. 6th, of the School Laws.

May combine schools.

Reg. 17. County Boards of Public Instruction are directed and enjoined to sub-divide their respective counties into convenient and permanent school districts, for each race separately, and to keep a record of each district by name, by number, and by description of lands contained therein (or by boundaries) in order that specific knowledge may be had as to the metes and bounds of each school district. It shall be the duty of said Boards to furnish each Supervisor with a proper description of the territory embraced within his jurisdiction.

To district counties.

To inform Supervisors of their jurisdiction.

Reg. 18. It shall be the duty of each County Board to adopt necessary regulations to restrict the attendance of pupils to the school within their own district, except as the Board may by special permit or by regulation allow attendance elsewhere; *Provided,* All pupils of the county, qualified therefor, may attend the County High School.

To restrict school attendance to proper district.

Reg. 19. County Boards of Public Instruction shall not enter into contract with any teacher for a term of service extending beyond the life of the certificate held by the teacher.

Not to contract for a term beyond the life of a certificate.

Reg. 20. County Boards of Public Instruction shall have the authority to remove any member of a Board of Trustees of a special tax school district who fails to discharge his duty.

To remove Trustees and appoint.

All vacancies in Boards of Trustees shall be filled for the unexpired term by the County Board of Public Instruction upon the nomination of the County Superintendent.

COUNTY SUPERINTENDENT OF PUBLIC INSTRCTION.

When to make annual report.

Reg. 21. The County Superintendent of Public Instruction in each county shall, not later than the fifteenth day of July of each year, prepare and forward to the State

Superintendent an Annual Report, .in conformity with
blanks and instructions sent out from the State Department.

1899.

REG. 22. The County Superintendent shall give ample
notice before every county examination of the time and
place thereof.

Notice of examinations.

REG. 23. In case separate places are necessary to be provided for the examination of white and negro teachers, the
County Superintendents are authorized to appoint competent
assistants to conduct the examinations, but he shall be responsible for the official acts of said assistants.

May appoint assistants.

REG. 24. County Superintendents are directed to furnish
the proper blanks, and to see that applicants for examination file the necessary endorsement of good moral character, as provided in section 61, before admitting them to the
examination.

To require endorsement of character.

REG. 25. In case a vacancy should occur in the teaching
force of any school between the regular meetings of the
Board, the County Superintendent is authorized to fill the
same, subject to the ratification of the Board at its next
regular meeting.

When to appoint teachers.

SEC. 26. County Superintendents shall direct teachers to
make out monthly reports for twenty days, and to instruct
teachers, in case a legal holiday falls within the month and
is not taught, to add as the attendance of that day the average attendance of the actual number of days taught that
month.

How to report holidays.

SUPERVISORS AND TRUSTEES.

REG. 27. School Supervisors shall be governed in the
general discharge of their duties by the directions and the
Rules and Regulations of the County Board of Public Instruction.

How governed.

REG. 28. The office of Supervisor is not one of control,
but of oversight only. Schools while in session are under
the immediate control of the County Board of Public Instruction. But in case of emergency the County Superintendent may suspend or close a school, subject to the action of the Board at its next meeting.

Powers defined.

Discretionary powers of County Superintendent.

Reg. 29. The patrons should recommend to the County Superintendent suitable persons for Supervisors (Sec. 40, Par. 3d); but the County Superintendent may exercise some discretion in nominating such to the Board of Public Instruction for appointment (Sec. 48, Par. 5th).

Trustees supersede Supervisors.

Reg. 30. The position of Supervisor is superseded by a Board of Trustees, when a school district becomes a sub-district [special tax district] and levies a special tax for school purposes. The duties prescribed for Supervisor shall then be performed by the Trustees.

TEACHERS.

Primary duties of teachers.

Reg. 31. Before beginning a school, a teacher must exhibit to the County Superintendent a certificate unimpaired by suspension, revocation or limitation, enter into a contract, procure a register and all necessary blanks. He must keep his register in accordance with the printed directions therein, and must make out his monthly reports in strict conformity to the blanks furnished.

Corporal punishment.

Reg. 32. Teachers are notified that there is nothing in the school laws of the State prohibiting the infliction of corporal punishment, when in their judgment it is necessary; *Provided, however,* That such punishment shall not be unnecessarily severe.

TEACHERS' CERTIFICATES.

Prerequisites for State Certificate.

Reg. 33. Applicants for examination for State Certificates, unless personally known to the State Superintendent, must file written evidence of having taught at least twenty-four (24) months under a county First Grade Certificate, or its equivalent, eight (8) months of which time must be shown to have been taught successfully in the schools of this State.

For Life Certificate.

Reg. 34. Applicants for Life Certificates must present endorsements in conformity to law, and in accordance with the blanks furnished by the State Superintendent.

Teachers should advance the grade of their certificate or be dropped out.

Reg. 35. "All teachers should of their own purpose seek from time to time to advance the class of their certificates by diligent and persistent study and the constant reading of the best journals of school work, and books treating of methods, discipline and government of the school, and so pass from the lowest to the highest grade of certificate, and carry with it the increased capacity for the true work of the school room.

County Superintendents discovering a disposition on the part of certain teachers to remain content with any certifi cate they may be fortunate enough to obtain, exhibiting no desire to rise higher or to become better qualified for their important work, should at once report the same to the Board of Public Instruction and recommend their removal from the corps of teachers in the county."—Hon. A. J. Russell, Reg. of 1891.

LIST OF FORMS

PRESCRIBED AND USED IN THE

Educational Department.

—

No. 1—Notice of Election as Member of County Board of Public Instruction.
2—Oath of Office of Member of County Board of Public Instruction.
3—Commission of an Elected Member of County Board of Public Instruction.
4—Commission of an Appointed Member of County Board of Public Instruction.
5—Acceptance of an Appointed Member of County Board of Public Instruction.
6—Removing Member of County Board of Public Instruction.
7—Recommending School Supervisor.
8—Appointment of School Supervisor.
9—Acceptance of Appointment as School Supervisor.
10—Notice of Election of School Trustees.
11—Commission of School Trustees.
12—Acceptance of School Trustees.
13—Endorsement of Applicant for County Examination.
14—Application for Examination for State Certificate.
15—Recommendation for Life Certificate.
16—Teacher's Third Grade Certificate.
17—Teacher's Second Grade Certificate.
18—Teacher's First Grade Certificate.
19—Teacher's State Certificate.
20—Teacher's Life Certificate.
21—Teacher's Temporary Certificate.
22—Suspension or Revocation of Teacher's Certificate.
23—Award of Board of Public Instruction on Charges Against Teacher on Appeal.
24—Contract with Teacher.

25—Teacher's Monthly Report.
26—Teacher's Final Report.
27—Notice of Suspension of Pupil by Teacher.
28—Notice for Special Meeting of Board.
29—Warrant on Treasurer of County Board of Public Instruction.
30—Notifying County Superintendent of Apportionment of School Fund.
31—Notifying Comptroller Who is Authorized to Receive County School Fund.
32—Requisition on Comptroller for School Fund Apportionment.
33—Bond of Trustees.
34—Contract for Building School House.
35—Deed by Husband and Wife to School Property.
36—Itemized Estimate by County Board of Public Instruction.
37—Itemized Estimate by Trustees.
38—Monthly Financial Statement of County Board.
39—Annual Report of County Superintendent. (*Omitted in this Compilation.*)
40—Teacher's Daily Register. (*Omitted*).

☞ County Superintendents must order these blanks by number, stating the number of each blank required.

FORMS.

No. 1.

Notice of Election as Member of County Board of Public Instruction.

Notice of Election.

OFFICE OF
STATE SUPERINTENDENT OF PUBLIC INSTRUCTION,
TALLAHASSEE, FLA.,...........190..

SIR--You have been elected to the office of *Member of the County Board of Public Instruction.*

If accepted, you will subscribe and execute the oath annexed to the Letter of Acceptance herewith transmitted. The oath may be taken before any Judge, Justice of the Peace, Clerk of Court, or Notary Public. On receipt of Oath of Office, your commission will be forwarded to you.

Very respectfully,

....

Secretary of State Board of Education and State Superintendent of Public Instruction.

To...................., Esq.

☞ Every school officer is required, before entering upon the duties of his office, and within ten days after receiving notice of his appointment, to subscribe to an acceptance of the appointment and to pledge that he will faithfully perform the duties of the position, and to forward the same with his post office address to the State Superintendent of Public Instruction.—*Revised Statutes, Section 232.*

No. 2.

Oath of Office of Member of County Board of Public Instruction.

OATH OF OFFICE.

STATE OF FLORIDA,
COUNTY OF...........

I do solemnly swear that I will support, protect and defend the Constitution and government of the United States and of the State of Florida against all enemies, domestic or foreign, and that I will bear true faith, loyalty and allegiance to the same, and that I am entitled to hold office under this Constitution, that I will well and faithfully perform all the duties of the office of Member of the Board of Public Instruction, in and for the above named county, on which I am now about to enter. So help me, God.

. . . .

. . . .

Sworn to and subscribed before me this . . . . day of . . . . 190 .

. . . .

. . . .

To . . . . , Secretary of the State Board of Education:

I accept the office of member of the Board of Public Instruction in and for the county of . . . . The above is the oath of office taken by me.

My School Board District is No . . . .
My Postoffice address is . . . .
                    Very respectfully,

. . . .

No. 3.

Commission of an Elected Member of County Board of Public Instruction.

DEPARTMENT OF PUBLIC INSTRUCTION, }
            STATE OF FLORIDA.   }

In the name and by the authority of the State of Florida:

WHEREAS, ... was duly elected on the . . . . day of . . . . , A. D. 190 . . , to be the member of the

County Board of Public Instruction in and for the county of
.............., from School Board District No ....., for the
term of two years from the first Tuesday after the first 'Monday in January, A. D. 190.., and until his successor be elected
and qualified according to Section 3, Chap. 4328, Laws of
Florida:

Now, therefore, I, ..., Superintendent
of Public Instruction for the State of Florida, under and by
virtue of the authority vested in me by the laws of the State,
and by Regulation No. 4 of the State Board of Education, do
hereby commission said .... to be a member of the
County Board of Public Instruction of .... county,
for the District and term aforesaid, to have, hold and exercise
the said office and all the powers appertaining thereto, and' to
perform the duties and receive the privileges and emoluments'
thereof, in accordance with the requirements of law.

In testimony whereof I do hereby set my hand and affix the
seal of the State Board of Education, at Talla-
[SEAL]   hassee, the Capital, this the ....day of............
A. D. 190..

................,
State Supt. Pub. Inst.

No. 4.
*Commission of an Appointed Member of County Board of
Public Instruction.*

OFFICE OF)
STATE BOARD OF EDUCATION OF FLORIDA, }
TALLAHASSEE, ..., 190..)

Mr. ....,
............, Fla.

SIR— You are hereby appointed by the State Board of Education of Florida to be a member of the Board of Public
Instruction for the county of ...., to fill the unexpired term of ...., member from school
Board District No. ...., of county aforesaid.

If accepted, notice of same must be returned on enclosed
blank within ten (10) days after receipt of appointment (Sec.
9, Par. 1st).

Very respectfully,
[SEAL]   ...., Secretary.

No. 5.

Acceptance of an Appointed Member of County Board of Public Instruction, County of........

STATE OF FLORIDA. }
........., 190.. }

To............,

Secretary State Board of Education.

Sir—I have the honor to accept the appointment by the State Board of Education to be a member of the County Board of Public Instruction for the county of............ from School Board District No.... of said county, and hereby pledge myself to perform faithfully and impartially the duties of the office. (Sec. 9, Par. 1st.)

Very respectfully,

No. 6.

Removing Member of County Board of Public Instruction.

OFFICE OF)
STATE BOARD OF EDUCATION OF FLORIDA, }
TALLAHASSEE,............, 190..)

To.............

.............:

Sir—For [state reason].............you are hereby removed from the County Board of Public Instruction for ....county.

Very respectfully,

....

President of Board.

................, Secretary.

No. 7.

Recommending School Supervisor.

.... (P. O.) FLA., }
.... 190.. }

To.....................
Co. Supt. Pub. Instruction.

SIR—Five days' notice of the time, place and purpose of the meeting having been given by the Supervisor, the patrons of school No. ...., at .... met and organized by the election of the undersigned as Chairman and Secretary.

After ballot of the patrons only, it was found that a majority favored the appointment of Mr. or Mrs...................,
of .... (P. O.), as Supervisor of said school. We hereby endorse.................. as a citizen of good moral character, temperate, upright, responsible, possessing a fair education, and as one who will perform the duties of the office impartially and faithfully.

..........................,
.... Chairman.
Secretary.

No. 8.

Appointment of School Supervisor.

OFFICE OF BOARD OF PUBLIC INSTRUCTION, }
COUNTY OF................, }
................, FLA., ..., 190.. }
To................,
....

SIR, OR MADAM—Having been duly recommended and endorsed as a suitable person to act as Supervisor of school No. ...., situated at ...., at a meeting of the Board of Public Instruction held on the....day of........, 190.., you were appointed accordingly (*for four years, or to fill the unexpired term of*), or during the faithful performance of the duties of the office.

Blank form of acceptance herewith enclosed must be signed and returned within ten (10) days, or the appointment will be considered rejected.

Very respectfully,
..........................,
Secretary and County Superintendent.

No. 9.

Acceptance of Appointment as School Supervisor.

..................., FLA., ⎱
.............., 190.. ⎰

To................... ...,

Sec. and Co. Supt. Pub. Inst.

Sir—I hereby accept the appointment as School Supervisor for School No...., situated at................, and pledge myself to perform all the duties of the office faithfully and impartially.

Very respectfully,

....

No. 10.

Notice of Election of School Trustees.

COUNTY OF............., 190.. ⎱
STATE OF FLORIDA, ⎰

To..................;

Co. Supt. and Sec. Board Pub. Inst.

Sir—WHEREAS, At an election, notice of which having been given as required by law for four consecutive weeks, ordered by the County Board of Public Instruction, and held on the......day of..........., A. D. 190.., to determine whether the territory fully described in a petition presented to said Board shall be a special tax school district, and for the election of three trustees therefor, and to determine the millage to be assessed and collected annually during the succeeding two years, a majority of the electors resident in said territory and qualified according to Section 7 of Chapter 4678, Laws of Florida, did vote to create such special tax school district and the district is established; therefore, we, the undersigned inspectors of said election, do recommend as entitled to receive commissions as trustees of said special tax school district No. ...., and otherwise known as .... school district, the three persons named below, because they received the highest number of votes cast for trustees at said election.

NAMES.	POST-OFFICE.
....	....
.	....
....	.

Signed. { .... } Inspectors of Election.

No. 11.

Commission of School Trustees.

COMMISSION OF TRUSTEE.

OFFICE OF THE BOARD OF PUBLIC INSTRUCTION, }
STATE OF FLORIDA, COUNTY OF ...., }
.................., ... 190.. }

To.................,
................, Fla.

Having been duly elected, on the....day of ....,
A. D. 190.., to be a member of the Board of Trustees in and
for special tax school district No.., otherwise known..... as
............School District, for the term of two years and
until your successor is elected and qualified according to
Chapter 4678, Lsws of Florida, you are hereby commissioned
to act as Trustee for said special tax school district during the
faithful and valuable performance of the duties which the
position devolves upon you—not to exceed two years, except
as provided herein.

A blank form of acceptance is herewith enclosed, which
please fill out and return within ten (10) days, or the position
will be declared vacant and filled by appointment

By order of the County Board of Public Instruction.

................,
Sec. and Co. Supt. Pub. Inst.

No. 12.

Acceptance of School Trustee.

COUNTY OF.............,
.... (P. O) ....190.. }

To................,
Sec. and Co. Supt. Pub. Inst.

SIR—I have received your letter of..................
enclosing commission of the Board of Public Instruction of this county as Trustee of special tax school District No...., called .... School District.

I hereby accept this position and pledge myself to perform its duties impartially and faithfully.

Very respectfully,

....

No. 13.

Endorsement of Applicant for County Examination.

.To................, ...,190.. }

Co. Supt. Pub, Inst.,
.... County.

SIR—This is to certify that I have been personally, acquainted with the bearer,............, for.........years and commend......to you as a person of good moral characacter, and addicted to no habits that could unfit or disqualify .... for the position of teacher.

Very respectfully,

....

No. 14.

Application for Examination for State Certificate.

.... FLA., }
.... 190.. }

To................,
State Supt. of Pub. Inst.

SIR—I hereby make application for examination for State

Certificate, and enclose herewith testimonials as to my character, and to my experience and success as a teacher.

Very respectfully,

....

Applicant must file endorsement from the school authorities under whom he has taught for the last twenty-four months (eight of which must have been in the schools of Florida), and said endorsement must certify to applicant's good moral character and success as a teacher.

No. 15.

Recommendation for Life Certificate.

.... Fla., }
.... 190.. }

To........... ....,

State Supt Pub. Inst.

Sir—We, the undersigned, each of us being a holder of a State Certificate granted in accordance with the provisions of Chapter 4192, Laws of Florida, and being well and personally acquainted with the work and character of.........., and having personally observed..... methods and noted........ success in the class room, both in the matter of instruction and discipline, do therefore endorse............. as a person possessing eminent teaching ability, and as having been eminently successful in governing and conducting a school, and as having taught successfully for the period of thirty (30) months in a High School in this State, and commend............. to you as a teacher worthy and well qualified in every respect to receive a Teacher's Life Certificate.

Very respectfully,

....

....

No. 16.

Teacher's Third Grade Certificate.

NOTE.—The different grades of Certificates are lithographed and issued in books of 100 each, with stubs. Stubs in all cases must be filled out as indicated.

STATE OF FLORIDA.

No........   [SEAL OF STATE.]   FOR 2 YEARS.

TEACHER'S CERTIFICATE—THIRD GRADE.

To the Board of Public Instruction of.............County:

This certifies that................ .....having presented the requisite endorsement of *good moral character*, and having been legally examined and found to possess the qualifications for *a Third Grade Teacher*, as prescribed in Section 1, Chapter 4331, an act to amend Chapter 4192, an act to provide for the *Uniform Examination of Teachers*, is hereby authorized to contract with your honorable Board, to teach in the public schools of this................county, for two years from this date.

Given under my hand this....day of............190..

. . . .

Supt. of Pub. Inst............Co.

Standing on examination, scale 100: Orthography....,'
Reading ...., History ...., Arithmetic ...., English Grammar ...., Geography ...., Composition ...., Physiology....,
Theory and Practice of Teaching ...., General Average ....

N. B.—No candidate can be awarded this certificate who fails to make a general average of 60 per cent., or falls in any branch below 40 per cent.

Form of Stub to Third Grade Certificate.

No....   Date or issue........, 190..   To..........
Sex........   Race........   Age.....   Home P. O........
Certificate expires...............
Standing on examination.
Scale 100.
(Same as in body of certificate).

No. 17:
Teacher's Second Grade Certificate.
STATE OF FLORIDA.

No   [SEAL OF THE STATE.]   FOR 3 YEARS.

TEACHER'S CERTIFICATE—SECOND GRADE.

To the Board of Public Instruction ....County:

This certifies that ....having presented the requisite endorsement of *good moral character*, and having been legally examined and found to possess the qualifications for a *Second Grade Teacher*, as prescribed in Section 2, Chapter 4331, an act to amend Chapter 4192, an act to provide for *Uniform Examination of Teachers*, is hereby authorized to contract with your honorable Board to teach in the public schools of this................county, for three years from this date.

Given under my hand this the ....day of.........190..

....
Supt. of Pub. Inst., ...Co.

Standing on examination. (Subjects same as for Third Grade). Scale 100.

N. B.—No candidate can be awarded this certificate who fails to make a general average of 75 per cent., or falls in any branch below 50 per cent.

It may be endorsed by any County Superintendent, and so endorsed becomes good for its unexpired term in such county. (*Vide Section* 8, *Chapter* 4331).

Form of Stub for Second Grade Certificate.

No.... Date of issue........, 190.. To..............
Sex....Race....Age.... Home P. O.... Has taught.. months....Last Certificate was.......Grade, Issued from.. county, Dated............ Standing on examination (Same as in body of certificate). Scale 100.

No. 18.
Teacher's First Grade Certificate.
STATE OF FLORIDA.

No..   [SEAL OF STATE.]   For Four Years.

TEACHER'S CERTIFICATE—FIRST GRADE.

To County Boards of Public Instruction, Greeting:

Be it known that........ having presented the requisite

endorsement of *good moral character*, and having passed satisfactory examination as prescribed in Sec. 3, Chap. 4331, an
act to amend Chapter 4192, an act to provide for the *Uniform
Examination of Teachers*, is therefore entitled to the rank of
First Grade Teacher, and is hereby licensed to teach in the
Public Schools of....... ..... county for the term of four
years from date.

Given under my hand this the......day of......, 190..
                        ...:.............
               Supt. of Pub. Inst............. Co.

Standing on examination, scale of 100.   Orthography ....,
Reading ...., U. S. History ...., Geography ...., English
Grammar ...., Arithmetic ...., Composition ...., Physiology ...., Theory and Practice of Teaching ...., Civil Government ...., Algebra ...., Physical Geography ...., General Average.

N. B.—This certificate may be endorsed upon the reverse
side by any County Superintendent, and so endorsed becomes
good for its unexpired term in such county. *Vide* Sec. 8,
Chap. 4331.

(The following will be contained in side stub to this certificate).

No.., Issued ...., 190.., To ...., Sex ...., Race ... , Age
...., Home P. O ...., No. months taught ...., Grade of last
Certificate...., Where issued, ..., Date of Same ...,
Standing on examination.
Scale 100.
(Same as in body of certificate).

———

No. 19.

Teacher's State Certificate.

STATE OF FLORIDA.

No..   [SEAL OF STATE.]   For Five Years.

TEACHER'S STATE CERTIFICATE.

OFFICE OF   '   ⎫
SUPERINTENDENT OF PUBLIC INSTRUCTION, ⎬
TALLAHASSEE, ..., 190..   ⎭

To County Boards of Public Instruction:

Whereas, The bearer .... has presented evidence to
show that .... has taught successfully at least twenty-

four months (eight or more of which in schools of Florida),
and that........is a person of good moral character, possessing ability to govern and aptness to teach, and has passed
satisfactory examination in the branches prescribed in Sec. 4,
Chap. 4331, an act to amend Chapter 4192, an act to provide
for the *Uniform Examination of Teachers* ....is hereby licensed to teach in any county in this State, and exempt
from further examination for five years from date.

Witness my hand and the Seal of the State Board of Education, this the....day of...., 190..

....
State Supt. Pub. Inst.

Standing on Examination, scale of 100. Geometry......,
Trigonometry...., Physics. .., Zoology...., Botany.·....,
Latin....., Rhetoric......, English Literature....., Mental
Science...., General History...., Average....

(The following is the side stub to this certificate).

State Certificate, No......, Date of issue......190.., To,
......., Sex...., Race...., Age...., Home P. O.........
Last Certificate was.......... Grade, Issued from..........
county, Dated......, Standing on examination.

(Same as in body of Certificate.)

No. 20.
Teacher's Life Certificate.

No.. STATE OF FLORIDA. Perpetual..

Teacher's Life [SEAL OF STATE.] Certificate..

Alios Docendo Discimus.

The eminent qualifications of.............as a teacher of
youth, having been shown by....distinguished success in the
schools of this State, and having presented the requisite endorsements and testimonials as provided by Sec. 5, Chap. 4331,
Laws of Florida,........is therefore awarded this Diploma
which is of perpetual validity, and forever exempts........
from further examination as a teacher in the public schools of
this State.

Given under my hand and the Seal of the State Board of
Education, at the city of Tallahassee, this the....day of....
190.. ....,
State Supt. Pub. Inst..

(Seal State Board of Education).

No. 21.

Teacher's Temporary Certificate.

OFFICE OF
SUPERINTENDENT OF PUBLIC INSTRUCTION,......COUNTY.
....190..

This is to certify, that............... having placed on
file in my office evidence of maintaining a good moral character, having furnished satisfactory reasons for having failed
to attend the regular examination, having fairly made the
grade on each branch recorded below in a special examination
conducted by me, and having, in addition thereto, manifested
considerable knowledge of the art of imparting instruction
and managing a school, is therefore granted this Teacher's
Temporary Certificate and is hereby authorized to teach the
public school No. ...., at .... in this county, only
until the first State examination.

STANDING IN THE EXAMINATION.

Orthography......Composition....Theory and Practice....
Reading..........U. S. History...Algebra..........
Arithmetic........Geography.....Civil Government. ...
English Grammar..Physiology.....General Average....
....
Co. Supt. Pub. Inst.

· N. B.—County Superintendents of Public Instruction will
issue this certificate to no applicant who fails to make the
minimum and average grade required for a Third Grade Certificate.

No. 22.

Suspension or Revocation of Teacher's Certificate.

OFFICE OF BOARD OF PUBLIC INSTRUCTION,
COUNTY.....................190..
To..............,
.............., Fla.

DEAR........—It is my unpleasant duty to inform you
that certain charges have been preferred against you, on appa-
rently sufficient grounds, alleging that (state the charges
plainly and briefly—see Section 48, Paragraph 13th,) in consequence of which your certificate to teach a public school is
hereby declared suspended (or revoked, as the case may be,)

and the right to teach a public school in this State, as well as the privileges conferred by said certificate, are suspended (or revoked, as the case may require), until further notice.

The case will be presented to the Board of Public Instruction, (or State Superintendent of Public Instruction, if the certificate had been issued by him; also state the time and place at which a hearing will be granted), at which time you shall have an opportunity to make a full and fair vindication of the charges, in conformity with the regulations of the Department of Public Instruction.

Very respectfully,

..................,

Co. Supt. of Pub. Inst.

No. 23.

Award of Board of Public Instruction on Charges Against a Teacher on Appeal.

OFFICE OF BOARD OF PUBLIC INSTRUCTION, }
COUNTY OF................,............, 190.. }

To.......................,

Teacher.

After a fair and careful examination, on appeal, of the charges preferred against you by .... to-wit: ....(recite the charges plainly and briefly), it appears to this Board that ...., (state the conclusion of the Board) you are hereby honorably acquitted and continued in your position in...........(or censured and discharged, as the case may be) the service of this Board. Your salary will be continued from the time of your suspension .... (or will not be continued, in case the suspension is confirmed or certificate revoked).

....................,

Chairman.

....,

Sec. and Co. Supt. Pub. Inst.

No. 24.

Contract with Teacher.

This contract, by and between.............Teacher, and the Board of Public Instruction for the county of.......... State of Florida, witnesseth:

That the said.................agree to teach the Public School No....at..............., or such other public school at the Board may elect, commencing on the..........day of............, 190.., for the term of..........months, and to perform well and faithfully the duties of teacher, according to the laws of the State and the Regulations of the Department of Public Instruction of Florida, and ·the Rules and Regulations of the Board of Public Instruction of.......... county.

The said Board of Public Instruction of................. county, for and in consideration of the services being so rendered, agrees to pay said.............the sum of......... dollars per school month, and to give such further aid as the law requires.

Provided, The Board may raise the salary or lengthen the term specified in this contract, or if the average attendance on such school for any month shall fall below..........per cent. of the largest enrollment during the school year, or if said teacher habitually fails to comply with the provisions of this contract, then the Board may lessen the salary, shorten the time specified herein, or annul this contract altogether.

Signed,

...................; Teacher.

.....................,

County Supt. and Secy.

By order of and for Co. Board Pub. Inst.

Witness ....

....

N. B.—The original must be filed in the office of the County Superintendent, who may give any teacher a duplicate on demand.

Teacher's Monthly Report.

Of School No..... situated at.......... county of........., for the month ending........ day of...., 190..

OF STUDIES PURSUED	NUMBER OF PUPILS IN EACH.	OF ATTENDANCE	ANSWER IN FIGURES.
		OF LEGAL PUPILS (Resident and between 6 and 21 years of age.)	
Chart Class........	....	Total number enrolled to date........	....
First Reader.......	....	Number of males enrolled to date........	....
Writing............	....	Number of females enrolled to date........	....
Orthography........	....	Aggregate days attendance for the month........	....
		Average daily attendance for the month........	....
Number Work........	....	Aggregate days attendance of males for the month........	....
		Average daily attendance of males for the month........	....
Second Reader......	....	Aggregate days attendance of females for the month........	....
Language Work......	....	Average daily attendance of females for the month........	....
Third Reader.......	....	Greatest number present any day during the month........	....
Geography..........	....	Number of cases of corporal punishment during the month........	....
Mental Arithmetic..	....	Number suspended or expelled during month........	....
Fourth Reader......	....	**ATTENDANCE OF ILLEGAL PUPILS.**	
Written Arithmetic.	....	Number under six years of age........	....
English Grammar....	....	Number over twenty-one years of age........	....
Fifth Reader.......	....	Number from other districts of the county........	....
U. S. History......	....	Number from other counties of the State........	....
Algebra............	....	Number from other States........	....
Physiology.........	....	**OF TIME.**	
Civil Government...	....	Number of days school has been taught during month........	....
General History ...	....	Number of days taught since beginning of school year........	....
Rhetoric	....	Number of days the Principal has actually taught during the month........	....
Geometry	....	Names of Assistants and number of days each has taught during the month........	....
Book-keeping. .. ··	....	....	....
Latin..............	....	....	....
Physics	....	....	....
Botany.............	....	....	....
Zoology	....	....	....
Other Studies......	....	....	....
Vocal Music	....	**OF VISITS.**	
Instrumental Music.	....	Number by County Superintendent	....
		Number by Supervisor or Trustees........	....

No. 26.

Teacher's Final Report for the School Year Ending June 30th, 190.., of School No. ...., Situated at
.................., Beginning ...., 190.., Closing ...., 190...
.....................County.

STATE OF FLORIDA....................

ATTENDANCE OF PUPILS.

	RESIDENTS.			NON-RESIDENTS.			REMARKS.
	Male.	Female.	Total.	Male.	Female.	Total.	
Total enrollment between 6 and 21 years of age not enrolled in another Public School this year. (See Rem. 1.)							1. Resident pupils are those living within the school district; non-residents, those living outside the school district.
Greatest number in attendance any one day..							2. Round by dividing the total attendance of each sex by the number of days school was taught.
Least number in attendance any one day....							
Average daily attendance for school year. (See Rem. 2.)							3. Average age reported under the head "Total" is found by dividing the sum of the ages of all the pupils by the number enrolled.
Average age of all pupils. [See Rem. 3.]							4. The total attendance of each sex is the aggregate days' attendance made by all pupils of that sex.
Total attendance. [See Rem. 4.]							

CLASSIFICATION OF ALL PUPILS.

	NUMBER.			AVERAGE AGE.			REMARKS.
	Male.	Female.	Total.	Male.	Female.	Total.	
Number in Chart or Beginners' Class. [See Rem. 5, (a)].							5. (a). Each pupil must be reported in only one class, the one he was in when school closed, or when he left school.
Number in First Reader Class..							
Number in Second Reader Class							
Number in Third Reader Class..							(b). Report in higher grades those in or beyond the Seventh Grade. Sixth Grade Studies: Orthography, Reading, Writing, Arithmetic, English Grammar, U. S. History, Geography, Composition and Elementary Physiology.
Number in Fourth Reader Class.							
Number in Fifth Reader Class...							
Number in Higher Grades than Fifth Reader Class. [See Rem. 5, (b)].							
Totals.....							

SCHOOL PROPERTY.

Kind of Building, Log, Brick or Frame.	No. Recitation Rooms in Buildings.	No. Patent Double Desks in House.	No. Patent Single Desks in House.	No. Square Yards Good Blackboard Surface.	VALUE OF		
					Lot	Buildings.	Furniture.	Apparatus.

TEACHERS.

Names of Teachers.	Sex.	Age.	No. Months taught in before this School.	Monthly Salary in Contract.	No. Days Paid for at this School	Grade of Present Certificate	In What County Issued.	DATE OF CERTIFICATE.		If a Graduate, From What Institution.
								Month.	Day.	Year.	

GENERAL QUESTIONS FOR COUNTY SUPERINTENDENT'S REPORT.

OF TIME.	OF PUPILS.		OF TEACHERS.	
	Male.	Female.	Male.	Female.

No. days your school was actually taught....................

No. holidays counted as taught........

No. visits by Supervisor or Trustees........

No. visits to your school by Co. Supt. one hour long or over........

No. pupils from other counties........

No. resident in other States......

No. taught under 6 years of age.

No. over 21 years of age........

No. of the above that attended a Training School for teachers last summer........

No. that attended the last State Teachers' Association........

No. that subscribe for an Educational Journal........

No. that take a State Educational Journal........

I certify that the above Report is faithfully and correctly made out.

............................., Principal.

No. 27.

Notice of Suspension of Pupil by Teacher.

SCHOOL NO . . . . ,   }
. . . ., 190 . .   }

To   . . . . ,

School Supervisor.

I regret to be compelled to inform you that under the provision of the school law (Section 73, Par. 5th), I have found it necessary, for the good of the school, to suspend . . . . (name pupil) from attendance at school for . . . . (not exceeding ten) days. The cause for such suspension is . . . . Have the kindness to call on me at your earliest convenience, to extend such aid and advice, and take such further action as you may judge proper, according to Section 75, Par. 3d, of the law.

Very respectfully,

. . . ., Teacher.

NOTE.—The teacher must also give immediate notice to the parents or guardian of the pupil, (Sec. 73, Par. 5th.) This *may* be done by modifying the above form, but is always *best* done in person.

At the interview, the teacher should carefully avoid finding needless fault with the child, and should manifest such kindly spirit toward both parent and child as should satisfy them that the suspension was not prompted by any malice, but only for the reformation of the pupil and the good of the school.

Indeed, a frank interview with the parent or guardian in advance of suspension would often render a resort to such a measure unnecessary.

In all cases of suspension, the teacher must report the matter, with the facts, both to the Supervisor and parent. The Supervisor must review all suspensions and report the same promptly to the County Superintendent, (Sec. 75, Par. 3d,) whose action on the matter shall be final.

No. 28.

Notice for Special Meeting of Board.

OFFICE OF
SUPERINTENDENT OF PUBLIC INSTRUCTION,
COUNTY OF................,
................, 190..

To.... ....,
Member County Board Public Instruction.

SIR—I have the honor to request your attendance at a special meeting of the County Board of Public Insruction, to be held at............, on the .... day of............, at the hour of .... (a. m. or p. m.), for the purpose of.... (state the object of the meeting).

..................,.
Co. Supt. Pub. Inst.

No. 29.

Warrant on Treasurer of County Board of Public Instruction.

STATE OF FLORIDA.

No.. TO THE TREASURER OF ....COUNTY BOARD OF PUBLIC INSTRUCTION.

Pay to the order of........ ...:...................
....Dollars.

[Seal of the State.]

From any moneys belonging to the County School Fund, for services as teacher in School No....at............Given at ...., Florida, this....day of .... 190..,
$........

Countersigned by

.............., ...,
Sec. and Co. Supt. Pub. Inst.   Chair. Co. Board Pub. Inst.

Form of Stub.

School Warrant. No...., $...., Issued............, 189..,
To............, Teacher of School No...., At.............
Payable out of County School Fund. For salary........
month. Received by me...............................

No. 30.

Notifying County Superintendent of Apportionment of School Funds.

EDUCATIONAL DEPARTMENT,)
STATE OF FLORIDA, -
TALLAHASSEE, ..., 190...)

DEAR SIR · The amount this day apportioned your county from the one mill tax (or interest on State School Fund) is $........

You will find the papers necessary for collection enclosed, which have properly signed and mailed to Hon..........., Comptroller.

Respectfully,
.............,
State Supt. Pub. Inst.

☞ Preserve this for your own information.

No. 31.

Notifying Comptroller who is Authorized to Receive County School Funds.

OFFICE OF)
BOARD PUBLIC INSTRTCTION, }
COUNTY OF............, }
............, 190..)

To Hon............, Comptroller, ·
Tallahassee, Fla.

SIR—This is to certify that .... is Treasurer of .... county, and is authorized to receive the sum apportioned to said county from the one mill tax (or interest on State School Fund) for the year 190..

..............,
Chairman Co. Board Pub. Inst.

..............,
Co. Supt. Pub. Inst.

No. 32.

Requisition on the Comptroller for School Fund Apportionment.

OFFICE OF
BOARD PUBLIC INSTRUCTION,
COUNTY OF ... ...,
................, 190..

To Hon. ...   ..., Comptroller,
                   Tallahassee, Fla.

SIR—We hereby make application for $......, the sum apportioned to .... county from the one mill tax (or terest on State School Fund) for the year 190..

................,
        Treasurer of........County.

..............,
   Chair. Co. Board Pub. Inst.

No. 33.
Bond of School Trustees.
(*Vide Sec 9, Par. 2d, this Compilation; Sec. 7, Chap.* 4336.)

Know all men by these presents, That we, A B, C D, and E F, Trustees of Special Tax School District No...county of......
State of Florida, as principals, and G H and J K, their sureties, are held and firmly bound unto the Board of Public Instruction of said county in the sum of (insert double the amount that will be liable to fall into their hands at any time) for the payment of which sum well and truly to be made, we firmly bind ourselves, our heirs, executors and administrators, jointly and severally, by these presents.

The condition of this obligation is such, that if the said A B, C D and E F, Trustees of Special Tax School District No....., county and State aforesaid, shall faithfully appropriate to their proper and lawful uses, as provided in Section 7, Chapter 4336, laws of 1895, all moneys or other property that may come into their hands by virtue of their office, and render promptly the required returns, and turn over to their successors all bonds, records and effects, then this obligation shall be void, otherwise of full force and virtue.

A B (Seal.)
C D (Seal.)
E F (Seal.)
G H (Seal.)
J K (Seal.)

No. 34.

Contract for Building School House.

STATE OF FLORIDA, ⎫
............COUNTY. ⎰   This contract made and entered into between A B of the county of........, State of Florida, and the Board of Public Instruction for the county of........., State of Florida, and their successors in office.

Witnesseth: That, in consideration of the sum of one dollar in hand paid to A B, the receipt whereof is hereby acknowledged, and of the further sum of....(insert total amount) to be paid as hereinafter provided, the said A B agrees to build a ....(describe the building here merely in general terms as log, frame, brick, etc.,) and furnish the material therefor, according to the plan and specifications for the construction of said house, hereunto appended, at........(describe the locality) and on such lot as the Board may direct.

The said house is to be built of the best material, in a substantial, workman-like manner, and is to be completed and delivered to the said Board, or their successors in office, free from any lien for work done or material furnished, by the........ day of............., 190..; and, in case the house is not finished and ready for delivery by the time herein specified, the said A B shall forfeit and pay to the said Board, or to their successors in office, for the use of the public schools of the county, the liquidated sum of.....(insert the forfeit money), and shall also be liable for all damages that may result to said Board in consequence of such failure.

The said Board hereby agrees for themselves, and their successors in office, to pay the said A B the sum of......dollars, when the said house is finished and delivered as herein stipulated; (or....dollars when the foundation of the house is ·finished; and the further sum of......dollars when the walls are up to the square and ready for the roof; the remaining sum of ......dollars when the said house is completed) as per plan and specification and keys are delivered.   ⸸

It is further agreed that this contract shall not be sub-let, transferred or assigned, without the mutual consent of both parties.

Witness our hands and seals this . . . . day of . . . . ,
A. D. 190 . .

. . . . ,
Contractor.

. . . . ,
Chair. Co. Board Pub. Inst.

. . . . ,
Sec. and Co. Supt. Pub. Inst.

Witness:

. . . .

. . . .

NOTE—Plans and specifications should be attached to the contract.

Boards should not attempt to build permanent and expensive school houses without getting some good mechanic or architect to draw up full and distinct plans and specifications.

Work on all school buildings should be done by contract and let to the lowest responsible bidder, and the money paid by the Board directly to the contractor himself.

No. 35.
Deed by Husband and Wife to School Property.

NOTE—It is the duty of County Boards of Public Instruction to obtain titles *in fee simple* to all school property. (Sec. 40, par. 1st.) The following form will answer in either case, whether the wife owns the property, or only signs to release dower.

STATE OF FLORIDA, }
. . . . COUNTY. } Know all men by these presents,
That we, A B and C D, his wife, of the county of . . . . ,
State of Florida, in consideration of the sum of . . . . . . dollars,
to us in hand paid, and by us received, do hereby bargain, sell,
grant and convey unto the Board of Public Instruction for the
county of . . . . , State of Florida, and to their successors
in office, the following described premises, situated in the
county and State aforesaid, to-wit: (Describe definitely the
premises by giving starting point, metes and bounds), together
with all the tenements, hereditaments and appurtenances
thereto belonging or in anywise appertaining, to have and to
hold in fee simple forever.

8

In witness whereof the said A B, as well as C D, his wife, who joins in this conveyance for the purpose of absolutely transferring all her claims to, and relinquishing and conveying all her estate and her right of dower in the above described premises, have hereunto set their hands and affixed their seals, this .... day of.........., in the year one thousand nine hundred and........

A B, (Seal.)
C D, (Seal.)

Signed, sealed and delivered
in presence of us—

....

....

STATE OF FLORIDA,)
..........COUNTY. {   I,........ .... a ....
(*Justice of the Peace, or Notary Public as the case may be*) in and for the State and county aforesaid, do hereby certify that on this ..... day of .... A. D. 190.. in said county, before me in person appeared *A B* and *C D*, his wife, both of them to me personally known, each of whom did duly and severally say and acknowledge before me that they and each of them did execute, sign, seal and deliver the foregoing deed of conveyance for the uses and purposes therein expressed. And the said Mrs. *C D*......, upon an examination had and made by me separately and apart from her said husband, did say and acknowledge before me that she executed, signed and sealed said deed for the purpose of absolutely conveying, releasing, relinquishing and renouncing all of her estate, right, title and interest in and to the land in said deed described, whether the same be dower interest or estate, or an independent separate estate in her own right, and that she did the same freely and voluntarily and without any compulsion, constraint, apprehension or fear of or from her said husband.

In witness whereof I hereunto, in the presence of the said acknowledgers, set my hand and seal the day and year above written.

A B .... (sign here).

C D .... (sign here).

.... [SEAL.]

(J. P. or Notary sign here, and attach private or official seal).

No. 36.

Itemized Estimate by County Board of Public Instruction.

OFFICE OF
BOARD OF PUBLIC INSTRUCTION,
.... COUNTY, June.., 190..

(*See Par.* 18*th, Sec.* 40.)

To Hon. ...., *Chairman, and Members of the Board*
of County Commissioners:

SIR—The County Board of Public Instruction in session on
this day found the following funds necessary for school operations in .... county for the school year beginning
July 1st, A. D. 190.., and ending June 30th, A. D. 190..

For payment of outstanding warrants........... $......
For purchase of text-books, charts, etc.... ....
For construction of school-houses........ ....
For rent of school-houses........ ....
For repair of school-houses.................... ....
For insurance of school-houses................. ......
For incidental expenses of schools ....
For furniture for schools..................... ......
For per diem and mileage of School Board...... .....
For incidental expenses of Board and Co. Supt... ......
For salary of County Superintendent of Schools.. ......
For salary of teachers of school No. 1 for....Mos. ......
For salary of teachers of school No. 2 for....Mos. ......
For salary of teachers of school No. 3 for....Mos. ......

(Complete list of schools).

Total.. $......

A levy of....mills on the taxable property of the county
will be necessary to give the amount imperatively needed, and
we hereby request you to levy the same,

By order of the County Board of Public Instruction.

..................,
Chairman Co. Board Pub. Inst.

..............,
Sec. and Co. Supt. Pub. Inst.

118   FORMS.

No. 37.

Itemized Estimate of School Trustees.

STATE OF FLORIDA,
SPECIAL SCHOOL TAX DISTRICT No...COUNTY OF........
...........(P. O.) June...., 190...

To Hon ...., Chairman, and Members Board County Commissioners.

SIRS—In compliance with Sec. 12, Chapter 4678, Laws of Florida, the School Trustees of Special Tax School District No. ......,known as ....District, hereby submit the following itemized estimate of school funds necessary to be levied as a special tax for the school year beginning July 1st, 190...:

No. miles *(Name the Railroad)* R. R. track in said district .... (Repeat twice the above line).

No. miles .... Telegraph lines in said district......... (Repeat above twice).

Amount necessary for new buildings............. $......
Amount necessary for repairs..................... ......
Amount necessary for rent of school buildings..... ......
Amoudt necessary for insurance.................. ......
Amount necessary for school libraries............ ......
Amount necessary for text-books................ ......
Amount necessary for salaries of teachers......... ......
Amount necessary for incidental expenses......... ......
Amount necessary for school furniture........... ......
Amount necessary for other school purposes....... ......

    Total................................. $.......

At an election held in said Special Tax School District on the ....day of........,190..., it was determined by a majority of those voting that a special tax of..... mills should be assessed and collected annually during the succeeding two years for school purposes, on the property of the Special Tax School District, bounded as follows: Beginning at northeast corner......, then run west along .... to ...., thence south along .... to ...., thence east along .... to ...., thence north along .... to starting point.

Your honorable body is hereby requested to make the above
levy.

Respectfully,

Signed.   .... ⎱
            .... ⎰ Trustees.
            ....

☞ A copy of the above must be filed with the Clerk of the
Board of County Commissioners, one with the Comptroller of.
the State, and one with the County Board of Public Instruction. See Sec. 12, Chapter 4678, Laws of Florida.

No. 38.

*Monthly Financial Statement of County Board of Public
Instruction*

STATE OF FLORIDA, ⎱
COUNTY OF........... ⎰
..............,........,190..

To Hon................,

Clerk Circuit Court.

SIR—In compliance with Section 2, Chapter 4332, Laws of
Florida, we hereby file with you the following itemized financial statement of all school moneys received, appropriations.
made and warrants issued for the month ending, the.........
day of..........., A. D. 199..

☞ In publishing, blank items may be omitted.

—o—

RECAPITULATION.

Total receipts during the month................... $......
Total expenditures during the month........... . $......

Balance in treasury..................... $......
Deficit in funds........................ $......

190...	ITEMIZED RECEIPTS.	
......	Balance in Treasury last report.............	$ ....
......	From Tax Collector, county School levy.....	......
......	" " " " " "	......
......	" " " poll tax....	......
......	" " " poll tax...............	......
......	" State Treasurer, redemption of lands...	......
......	" " " one mill tax............	......
......	" " " school fund interest......	......
......	" County Supt., tuition non-resident pupils	......
......	" " " examination fees.........	......
.... *	"	......
......	"	......
	Total receipts.................	.....

*Here state amount from other sources.

ITEMIZED EXPENDITURES.

Warrant Number.	To Whom.	For What.	Date.	Amount.
64	Jonn Doe ..	Salary as Teacher.......	Oct. 3, 1895	$40 00
		(The above is sample of entry This space may be extended to suit requirements.)		
...	....	Salary County Superintendent	....	....
...	....	Traveling exnenses Co. Supt..	... .	......
.. .	....	Per diem and mileage as member of Board.....	....	.....
....	....	" " "		
		" " "		
....	....	Office expenses of County Superintendent and Board	....	.....
......	....	School lot at..........No....	....	.....
....	....	Building school house at......	....	.....
....	....	No.......... " " "		
		" " "		

...	....	Repairs on school building at		
....	....	..............No.	....	......
		" " "		
		" " "		
....	....	Rent of school building at...		
....	....	.............No.	....	......
		" " "		
		" " "		
....	....	Insurance of school building at		
....	....	.............No.	....	......
		" " "		
		" " "		
...	....	Fuel for school No....at.....	....	.....
		" " "		
		" " "		
....	....	Janitor for school No ..at....	....	......
		" " "		
		" " "		
....	....	Furniture for school No.		
....	....	at........ ....'......	....	.....
		" " "		
		" " "		
...	....	Commission of Treasurer.....	....	... ..
...	....	County school debt...........	....	......
...	....	Interest on indebtedness	.. ..	....
...	....	Pupils attending school in ..	....	... ..
..	....	... ... county	....	... ..
		" " "		
		" " "		
....	....	Institutes or Summer Schools.	....	.....
. ..	....	Service on Grading Committee.	....	.....
		" " "		
		" " "		
....	....	Free text books.......	....	......
....	....	*...............	....	....
....	....	....	....	... ..
....	....	....	....	... ..
....	....	....	....	... ...
		Total expenditures........	....	......

*Here state amounts for other purposes.

APPROPRIATIONS.

For School No. 1, salary of teacher for........Mos...|$....
For School No. 2, salary of teacher for.......Mos...| ....

(*Complete List*).

For salary of County Superintendent per annum............|....
For traveling expenses of County Superintendent......|....
For per diem and mileage County Board...............|....
For school lot at...................................|....
   "   "   "   ....|....
   "   "   "   ....|....
For building school house at......................|....
   "   "   "   "   ....|....
   "   "   "   "   ....|....
For repairs on school at..........................|....
   "   "   "   "   ....|....
   "   "   "   "   ....|....
For furniture for school at.......................|....
   "   "   "   "   ....|....
   "   "   "   "   ....|....
For fuel for school at...... ....|....
   "   "   "   "   ....|....
   "   "   "   "   ....|....
For insurance of school house at..................|....
   "   "   "   "   ....|....
   "   "   "   "   ....|....
For janitor for school at.........................|....
   "   "   "   "   ....|....
   "   "   "   "   ....|....
For county school indebtedness....................|....
For interest on indebtedness......................|....
For pupils attending schools in other counties.....|....
For commissions of Treasurer......................|....
For office expenses of County Superintendent and Board.|....
For Institutes or Summer Schools.... ....|....
For expenses of examinations......................|....
For free text-books...............................|....
* ....|....
....|....
....|....
....|....
....|....

       Total appropriations.......................|....

   *Other purposes, state what.

(Endorsement for Back of this Form.)

FINANCIAL STATEMENT.

OF

BOARD OF PUBLIC INSTRUCTION

OF

.... County.

For month ending .... day of .... 190..

FILED WITH CLERK OF CIRCUIT COURT, the......day of....
.....................190..

We certify that the within statement is true and correct in every particular.

..................,
Chairman Co. Board Pub. Inst.

Attest:

..................,
Co. Supt. Pub. Inst.

INDEX.

A.

9

134   INDEX.

146   INDEX.

10

S.

T.